RUN AS ONE

Great Plains Publications gratefully acknowledges the financial support provided for
its publishing program by the Government of Canada through the Canada Book Fund;
the Canada Council for the Arts; the Province of Manitoba through the Book Publishing
Tax Credit and the Book Publisher Marketing Assistance Program; and the Manitoba
Arts Council.

Design & Typography by Relish New Brand Experience
Printed in Canada by Friesens
Photos courtesy Errol Ranville

LIBRARY AND ARCHIVES CANADA CATALOGUING IN PUBLICATION

Title: Run as one : my story / Errol Ranville.
Names: Ranville, Errol, 1953- author.
Identifiers: Canadiana (print) 2021010788X | Canadiana (ebook) 20210107944 |
   ISBN 9781773370606 (softcover) | ISBN 9781773370613 (ebook)
Subjects: LCSH: Ranville, Errol, 1953- | LCSH: C-Weed Band. | LCSH: Country
   musicians—Canada—Biography. | CSH: Indigenous musicians—Canada—Biography. |
   LCGFT: Autobiographies.
Classification: LCC ML420.R213 A3 2021 | DDC 782.421642092—dc23

ENVIRONMENTAL BENEFITS STATEMENT

Great Plains Publications saved the following
resources by printing the pages of this book on
chlorine free paper made with 100% post-consumer
waste.

TREES	WATER	ENERGY	SOLID WASTE	GREENHOUSE GASES
13	1,000	5	43	5,460
FULLY GROWN	GALLONS	MILLION BTUs	POUNDS	POUNDS

Environmental impact estimates were made using the Environmental Paper Network
Paper Calculator 4.0. For more information visit www.papercalculator.org.

Canadä

FSC
www.fsc.org
MIX
Paper from
responsible sources
FSC® C016245

RUN
AS
ONE
MY STORY

ERROL 'C-WEED' RANVILLE
WITH JOHN EINARSON

GREAT PLAINS
PUBLICATIONS

CONTENTS

This book is dedicated to our late brother Bryan Ranville.
Our spin doctor and we sure miss you now.

FOREWORD

In the pantheon of Indigenous music, there are few who have broken the barriers that kept them confined to finding favour solely with an Indigenous audience. Few have carved themselves a name that qualifies as Legend. Errol Ranville is certainly that, and yet he remains down-to-earth and stays true to himself as he remains close to his roots. As one of the most prolific Indigenous artists that has ever come from Turtle Island, Mr. Ranville is still as relevant today as he was when his record first climbed to number one in the nation some forty years ago. Hailing from the dusty roads of Eddystone, Manitoba, this legend has crisscrossed North America and has graced the stages of Europe and China. Errol's story has been a long time in coming.

As a teenager, I first saw Errol coming to my home reserve by boat. We had no roads leading into our community at the time. Errol and his C-Weed bandmates had their gear in tow, and back then, every time a boat came in from the outside world, we would be curious as to who was coming in and what they were coming to do in our reserve. The C-Weed Band had arrived to play in our local band hall at the request of our Chief at the time.

Excitement filled the air. Everyone had already been hearing the song "Evangeline" on the local radio station at least twenty times a day. I was thirteen years of age and experiencing my first encounter with the C-Weed Band.

Since that time, I have followed their career. I have seen them on TV and have always been proud that this group of Indigenous musicians was playing more than just band halls. They have played on the same stages with the best artists in the country. Throughout the years, the men in C-Weed became good friends of mine. From the beginning, I have always been a fan. Today, you won't always find me in the crowd at their shows—you'll see me living my dream performing on stage with them—one of the greatest things I have ever experienced.

I once helped to organize a trip from Brandon University to Winnipeg to attend a protest. Our Chiefs in Manitoba were standing up against legislation they did not agree with. The protest march was set to begin at the Oodena Circle at The Forks. The Chiefs were lined up and ready to go. Before they started their march, the C-Weed Band launched into the most powerful send-off that I have ever experienced. Drumming began and was accompanied by powerful pow-wow singing, as a catchy guitar riff launched the indelible song "Run as One." I stood there just taking in this moment, realizing that this is one of the greatest anthems of the Indigenous protest movement that we have ever been gifted. This powerful song came through Errol Ranville.

I cannot remember a time when I have been so proud of being who I was as a Cree man. This song made me proud of who we are as the Indigenous people of this land. I marched with pride that day and I still do, to this day.

Years later, I became Chief of my First Nation. We invited C-Weed to come and play at our festivals. I became a host to them and spent time with them. I always had a good time with these men, the finest musicians that came from our people. Not only are they fine musicians, but they carry themselves with humility. Their attitude of respect is genuine, and I admire that.

At least twelve years ago, I was befriended by Errol and we have been close friends ever since. I continue to be impressed by his demeanor and his character. He has never tried to be cool or tried to impress anyone; he just blended into any environment in which he found himself.

When I talk about my relationship with Errol, I always mention how well-informed he is about politics. He is extremely well-read on many issues that matter to our people. I always talk proudly of his commitment to his sobriety and drug-free life, and how his spirituality is personal, but runs deep in his soul.

Many hours of driving around, enjoying suppers together, and talking about everything under the sun—this is one of the things I am most thankful for in my life. Hanging around, listening to him talk, and knowing that he is probably one of the few people who thinks I'm funny makes me cherish the brother I have found in him. I am very privileged to be counted as one of those in his inner circle.

I have heard many stories of the triumphs and the tragedies on his journey in life, and most of them were over a kitchen table or at times driving to a concert to which he had invited me. I am glad he is finally telling his stories, because they need to be told. They must be told. Errol's story is one of love and loss, and one that is painful to tell. It is a miraculous story to say the least.

If I were to define Errol Ranville in three words, those words would be: visionary, troubadour, and warrior.

Grand Chief Garrison Settee
Manitoba Keewatinowi Okimakanak

NOTE FROM PHIL FONTAINE

The C-Weed Band has been a mainstay on the Canadian music scene for almost four decades. Led by the immensely talented Errol Ranville, the C-Weed Band has played in Indigenous communities and in cities across the country for the enjoyment of Canadians from all walks of life.

Errol Ranville was born into a large musical family in Eddystone/Ste. Rose du Lac, Manitoba. He picked up the guitar as a child and never put it down. Taking the stage for the first time at eight years old, Errol found confidence and happiness playing in front of an audience. Errol established the C-Weed Band in 1965 and went on to achieve a loyal following and recognition by way of multiple Juno nominations in 1985 and 1986. Errol created the new C-Weed Band in the late 1990s and went on to release their successful *Run as One* album, which gained widespread recognition for its unique mix of mainstream music with traditional drumming and chanting. *Run as One* was such a huge hit that it received a Juno nomination in 2001, solidifying the place of C-Weed and Errol Ranville in the annals of Canadian music history.

The C-Weed Band is unique. The incredible story of Errol Ranville and his development as a musician from childhood to adulthood is a wonderful story. Errol is a self-taught musician who has spent a significant part of his life working to showcase the talents of other Indigenous musical artists. In 2005, Errol was inducted into the

Aboriginal Music Hall of Fame and in 2011 he received the Lifetime Achievement Award during the Aboriginal Peoples Choice Music Awards. Nineteen albums and almost four decades later, the C-Weed Band shows no sign of slowing down. They remain as popular as ever. Their enduring popularity can be traced to their undeniable talents as well as their ability to evolve over time.

The story behind the C-Weed Band is interesting, with as many twists and turns as that of any band of such longevity. It is about the love of music, the love of entertaining, and the growth of individuals as musicians over time, but also the growth of individuals in understanding themselves and their cultures. Throughout the many years of making music and playing for live audiences, the C-Weed Band remains committed to making good music and to bringing Indigenous music into the mainstream. The C-Weed Band is quite simply a great Canadian country band.

Phil Fontaine
Former Grand Chief of the Assembly of First Nations

NOTE FROM ERIC ROBINSON

I first met Errol in the early 1970s when we were both 17 years old. Both of us had somehow made our way into the City of Winnipeg from our home communities. At the time he was playing with his brothers in what became the C-Weed Band, the host band at the old Brunswick Hotel. Back then if you wanted to find somebody from up North all you had to do was take a stroll down the Main Street strip. Even as a teenager the talent in Errol was undeniable and this is where he started building his massive fan base.

Known for his talent nationwide and around the world, Errol Ranville is one of the pioneers of the music industry here in Manitoba. Although we lost touch for some time after our teenage years, I always followed his music through my work as a radio host in stations across the country. During those years we both became sober, became fathers and built our careers until our paths eventually crossed again in the early 2000s. When we were reacquainted, I was a Minister of the Crown for the Province of Manitoba. As the Minister of Culture, it was my duty to fund arts opportunities for all Manitobans. It was then that I asked Errol to come work for the province as the Aboriginal Music Coordinator. I remember shaking his hand and saying, "Let's make Winnipeg the Chicago of the North for our artists."

I have a great respect for Errol as a friend and brother, he is the kind of person who will help musicians build their talent, hone their skills and find their voice. One thing I truly admire is his ability to help people who are struggling with addictions by just being a supportive presence in their lives. The highlight of our many years of friendship was the day I was honoured with the duty of performing his marriage to the love of his life Marcie. The hardest moment of our friendship was the day that I had to officiate her funeral.

I would like to note that it was Errol, myself, my daughter and other visionaries who founded the Manito Ahbee Festival of Nations. This has given hundreds of Indigenous artists from Turtle Island and abroad an opportunity to showcase their music over the years. I am very proud of that fact and I think it is a huge accomplishment for a couple of guys who drank beer together on the main streets of Winnipeg so many years ago.

Indeed, a lot has happened over the years and I am honoured to have been asked to write this forward for my friend. I am so proud of your work Errol and I wish you continued success and good health. Keep making music and fly like a free bird, brother.

The Hon. Eric Robinson
Former Manitoba Minister of Cultural and Heritage

Walk Me to The Edge

It's a smell that never leaves you, the smell of burning flesh. Police officers and firefighters will tell you that. Months after the October 2010 highway accident that took five lives, including my beloved wife, Marcie, I would wake up in a cold sweat in the middle of the night and I could smell it in my nostrils. I could taste the smoke in the bottom of my throat and hear the fire raging in my ears. I would also hear Marcie laughing in the kitchen, talking to someone. Sitting up in bed, I would strain to hear what was going on. I had left the hospital in a wheelchair, but when you wake up from a dead sleep and hear voices in the next room, you forget that you can't walk. So, when I would jump out of bed to go see Marcie, I fell face down on the hard floor. The voices appeared to get louder and I recognized Marcie's laugh, so I would crawl as fast as I could to the doorway, poke my head out the bedroom, and peer down the darkened hallway. But she was not there. It was deathly quiet; nobody was there, and the pain from my fall from the bed started to set in. I knew I would struggle a long time to get back up and into bed. I started to cry. Convulsive crying, like I would never be able to stop.

Like a war veteran, I suffered from PTSD, Post Traumatic Stress Disorder. I would wake up in the middle of the night screaming to save Marcie. I would hear my dog Max, who had also perished in the accident, walking around in the next room, his nails hitting the hardwood floor. Again, I would jump out of bed and hit the deck, this time seriously hurting my elbow trying to break the fall then crawl as fast as I could again out into the hallway, but Max was not there. It was so very quiet and dark in our house.

It compounded my depression over her death. I became a recluse in my house, afraid to venture outside, dwelling over my loss. I am a survivor, but it would take all the inner strength I could muster to put the nightmares behind me.

It had all happened in a matter of seconds. Once Marcie and I spotted the oncoming vehicle with no lights on bearing down on us in our traffic lane, there was no time to react. No sooner had we seen them when they hit us head on, full speed both vehicles. No time to brake. I looked over at Marcie. It's a scene I'll never be able to forget. The engine had been pushed full on into her lifeless body. I tried unsuccessfully to unbuckle her and save her knowing in my heart she was already gone. At least she never suffered.

My own life was saved by two truck drivers passing by who saw the damaged vehicles and the fire. They pulled me out of a watery ditch that I had managed to crawl into after escaping from our burning Jeep. I would have drowned if they hadn't acted quickly. It could have been six deaths out on Provincial Highway #10 in northern Manitoba.

The accident made the newspapers and television news the following day. Four Indigenous youth and one white woman killed instantly in a head-on collision just two miles south of The Pas. Of course, my name was prominent since I was recognizable in the entertainment and recording community and was a two-time Juno Award nominee. I was scheduled to play the Aseneskak Casino with my band, The C-Weed Band. I never made it. Instead, I spent almost a year recovering from a crushed right ankle and broken bones in my left ankle, a damaged lumbar 5 in my back, and respiratory problems as a result of a damaged sternum. Doctors weren't sure at first if I would survive the injuries. I was hospitalized for sixty-six days. I'm very fortunate and very thankful.

Worse still, a year after the accident the provincial justice system charged me with careless driving. By making it a lower charge of careless driving, I think they hoped I would plead guilty and then they would evade liability for the accident. The whole ploy was to escape liability. I believed that the RCMP, University of the North, and Manitoba highways would all become liable for the accident unless they could determine a cause of the accident that they could assign blame and get themselves off the hook.

The battles with the RCMP, my lawyers, the provincial justice system, and Manitoba Public Insurance (MPI) were frustrating and debilitating. The cornerstone of our legal system is the notion of innocent until proven guilty. You don't have to prove your innocence; the onus is on the Crown or prosecution to prove your guilt. But for Indigenous people it's the other way around. You're guilty, and must try to prove your innocence in a system stacked against you. In the end it cost me well over $50,000 to prove I was not responsible for the accident. Not many Indigenous people can afford to do that. Again, I have been fortunate.

Lying in my hospital bed I was overwhelmed by the number of visitors who came with well-wishes. Musicians who knew first-hand the perils of a life on the road came to give me encouragement for my long recovery ahead. We are all brothers of the road. At one point the lineup of people was all the way down the hall to the elevator. Several leaders in the Indigenous community were among the visitors. They offered me emotional and spiritual support. They also agreed that while this was a tragic accident that took the lives of five people, I survived for a reason. God had spared me. Why? They told me I needed to find out what that reason was and pursue it.

CHAPTER 1

Magic In The Music

Errol was pretty off the wall as a youngster, kind of full of himself, rambunctious, full of energy, scrappy. He would get into fights at school. He even had a fight with a teacher once, a physical fight. He challenged authority. He still does. He had a lot of nerve, a lot of guts, and this carried through into his adult life and probably had a lot to do with his success and the success of the band. He is very driven.
—*Wally Ranville, brother*

I was in school with Errol. It was a two-room school, grades 5 to 8 in one room and grades 1 to 4 in the other. The principal had left so the teacher in grades 1 to 4 became sort of the head of the school. She was a bit strap happy and tended to give the strap for a lot of things. And I guess the grade 8 boys had done something, I cannot even recall what it was, so she brought them all in and stood them in the back of our room. We were all seated in our chairs. One by one they held out their hands and she gave them the strap. Whack! Errol was in the middle of the lineup. When she came to him, he moved his hand and she hit her leg. She got angry. We didn't know whether to laugh or what exactly to do. She put her hand out to hold his and of course he just yanked his hand out and she slapped her hand. Now she was furious. I cannot really recall what happened after but what sticks in my mind is he actually stood up to her because she gave the strap for no apparent good reasons. He wasn't going to take that from anyone. That's the kind of person Errol was.—*Curtis Johnson, Eddystone resident*

Running. I've been running all my life. Running from chronic poverty and racism in rural Manitoba, from a discriminatory music business that told us "We don't want your kind here," from people trying to label me and my music, from alcohol and drug addiction, from the responsibilities that come with being regarded as a role model. And running from a horrific accident that took away the love of my life, leaving me both physically and emotionally broken. Running is in my DNA. I read a saying once: "The only way I am ever going to get to go to Heaven is by running away from Hell." That saying sure applies to me and my current situation. A man on the run.

The name Ranville originates from France; Normandy to be precise. Ranville is a town on the northwest French coast that was liberated from German occupation by the Allies on D-Day, June 6, 1945. It was the first French community to be liberated. There is a Commonwealth cemetery situated up from the beach called Ranville Cemetery. The town dates back to Roman times. My brother Bryan, the family historian, traced our family roots back to 16th century France. Jean De Rainville and his wife Elizabeth De La Gueripierre emigrated to North America around 1678, settling in New France (Quebec). On arrival somehow the name was recorded as Rainville, dropping the De. Their occupation was listed as fur traders and subsequent generations included voyageurs who made the arduous canoe journeys west to trade with the Indigenous peoples. In 1753, Joseph Rainville (Renville) married Miniyuhe, daughter of Mdwakanton Dakota Chief Big Thunder of the Kaposia Village near Lower Agency Reserve in Minnesota and settled in what is now northern Minnesota.

From this, the town of Renville grew. Further intermarriage with Sioux tribes led to the Renville family extending into Montana and as far north as Pembina, North Dakota. Joseph Renville, the son of Joseph Rainville above, (whose name was later changed to Renville), in 1804 married Marie (Tonkanne) Little Crow, the daughter of Petit Carboneau and the niece of Chief Little Crow. On the July 3, 1823, Joseph joined Major Stevens H. Long's expedition to the source of the St. Peters River. He was highly valued and was chosen by Colonel Dickson to command the Sioux contingent of the expedition at the rank equivalent to a Captain in the British Army. By the time the American Fur Company bought the Columbia Fur Company, Joseph was established at Lac Qui Parle and maintained an army of warriors known as the Tokadantee or "Prairie Dogs." This group later evolved into the Renville Rangers under one of his sons. The Renville Rangers were an Indigenous group on horseback who kept the peace between the white settlers and the Sioux tribes in Minnesota.

There was no firm border yet and Indigenous people moved back and forth. But once the 49th parallel was set as the dividing line between British North America (Canada) and the United States, Renville and its occupants, including my mixed-marriage ancestors, found themselves on the American side. My father is American Sioux and a direct descendant of the Renville Rangers. It's a proud history.

Around 1862 an uprising alternately known as the Sioux Uprising or the Dakota Conflict arose from the ill treatment of the Sioux and Dakota tribes by the American government. Starvation was rampant as the government failed to adequately provide sufficient supplies to the Indigenous communities according to the treaties that had been negotiated by Dakota Chief Little Crow. In response, several white settlements were raided. The American response was heavy handed. The military captured and interned hundreds of Indigenous people and over three hundred were sentenced to death. On December 26, 1862 at Fort Ulm near Mankato, Minnesota, thirty-eight Sioux and Dakota were hanged in the largest mass execution in American history. Four of those hanged were direct descendants of my family. Fearful for their own safety, my father's family managed to escape across the Canadian border. Running from the hangman. But despite finding refuge in Canada, that fear never left them and continued to impact successive generations in Canada, including my father. They took the name Ranville to avoid being caught and did not register with the Canadian government for fear of being deported back to the US to be hanged. They lived their entire lives outside the treaties and never registered under the Indian Act. My great-grandfather, Jonas Ranville, who is my father's grandfather, was the first of our family to come across to Canada. Jonas Ranville is the father-in-law of Métis leader and Father of Manitoba, Louis Riel. He gave refuge to Louis Riel when he hid in the US for a period of time.

My grandfather Francois 'Frank' Ranville, born in 1882, didn't feel comfortable living close to the American border so he went north of Dauphin to Crane River. There he came across a priest who had a twelve-year-old girl, Henrietta Nepinak, a Treaty Indian from Pine Creek, under his care after she had caused some commotion in the community. Frank worked all summer clearing the property around the church and building a white picket fence. At the end of the summer, the priest had no money to pay him so he gave Frank the girl. Frank and Henrietta married in 1915 in Pine Creek and had twenty children of which seventeen lived to adulthood. One of them was my father, Emile Ranville, born on March 29, 1919 in Crane River. Frank went on to own a large cattle ranch and was respected in the community.

A river divided my grandfather's land, known as Ranville Point (Big Sandy Point), from the rest of the community. When the federal government Indian agents would come around to register the Indigenous members of the community around Crane River for their treaty rights and give them new English names and provisions like bread and sugar, my grandfather refused to cross the river. He didn't want to be registered because he feared that once they knew who he

was, they would send him back to the United States. He never registered with the Canadian government. That is why we slipped through
the cracks and lost our treaty rights. He lived his whole life in fear
of the hangman, my dad and his dad. They were outlaws running
from the kangaroo courts that were being held along the Minnesota
border in 1863 and randomly hanging Sioux Indians as a result of
the so called "Sioux uprising of 1862." In the 1863 operations against
the Sioux in North Dakota, Colonel Sibley, with two thousand men,
hunted the Sioux into Dakota Territory, by 1881, the majority of
the Sioux had surrendered to American military forces. In 1890, the
Wounded Knee Massacre ended all effective Sioux resistance to the
settlers on our land.

I lived outside the treaties all my life. I never had a status card.
We lived our whole life as Métis. Later, with the C-Weed Band, I
often had difficulty crossing the US border because of my lack of
status as a Treaty Indian. But after I turned sixty, the federal government announced Bill-C31, which stated that if your grandmother was
treaty then you could apply for treaty rights. Henrietta Ranville (nee
Nepinak), my grandmother, was a treaty Indian of the Pine Creek
First Nation. But I had to jump through all sorts of legal hoops before
sending off my application to Ottawa. A few months later I received
my card in the mail. It's now official. After sixty years, POOF, I'm
now an Indian. The first thing I did was go out and buy a brand-new
Chevy Suburban and with my Status card saved the sales taxes on it,
$5700. It's a small price to pay for giving up the land mass known as
Canada or Kanata.

My dad, Emile, was living in the small town of Eddystone, east of
Ste. Rose du Lac and north of Ebb and Flow First Nation. He had
left his father's cattle ranch to strike out on his own. With sixteen
siblings he wasn't going to inherit anything. Dad was a jack-of-all-
trades labourer. He could do just about anything, notably carpentry.

While working in Eddystone, he met Mary Catherine Spence, born April 24, 1912, the daughter of Joseph Spence, who my father was working for. She was twenty-nine and unmarried; he was twenty-two. They wed on September 29, 1940 in Winnipeg where Dad was working in a meat-packing plant. They operated a rooming house on Broadway in Winnipeg.

Dad was functionally illiterate. He never learned to read or write. When growing up, he spoke what was referred to then as "mud French," a conversational French/Cree derivative. Cree was his second language, Saulteaux his third, and around age seventeen he learned English. My parents could both speak Saulteaux but didn't dare do so. Like his father and grandfather, Emile remained fearful of the government sending him to the States, so he insisted we only speak English. The Canadian government had banned the use of our Native languages. If you were caught speaking your language at school, you would be suspended for two weeks. If you were caught a second time the suspension would double to one month and so on. So Indigenous kids would fail their grade that year because they would get behind and couldn't catch up. The following year they would then be in a class with kids a year younger than themselves, would become discouraged, and ultimately quit.

Because Dad had no carpentry license and couldn't read or write, he was often taken advantage of by local businessmen. He would be paid less because they knew they could get away with it. He wasn't going to dispute the wages because he didn't want to involve the government, once again from fear of deportation. Sometimes things turned ugly when alcohol was involved and there would be physical altercations. He worked hard all his life. He had to, as the family grew to twelve children. He instilled in all of us a strong work ethic. You don't get anything free; you have to work for it. Mom could read and write because she had been educated at a residential school. She was raised Catholic and was extremely religious. We went to church every Sunday until one by one we gradually stopped. But my father wasn't religious. Far from it. He never went to church. Once I snuck out of church one Sunday morning and went back home. I looked in the window and there was Dad, sitting all by himself in the house. The whole community would be at church and he'd be sitting alone on the bench. He used to say, "God's not going to put food on this table. If I don't go out and work, we won't have any food on the table!" I couldn't argue with that.

I loved my dad. He was my hero. He passed away in 1990, Mom in 1995.

My oldest siblings Valerie (born 1942), Stirling (born 1944), Delphine (born 1946), Gerald Bryan (known all his life as D-Bine born 1948), Gordon Nelson (born 1949) were all born while the family lived in Winnipeg, but soon after, Emile and Mary moved back to Eddystone. There wasn't much in Eddystone then: a post office, general store run by the Johnsons, a school, church, later a garage, and a mud trail to Crane River a few miles north up the road. We didn't own any land. When the local municipality would build gravel roads back then, they had something called a road allowance, the land between the road itself and where the farmers fences started. Dad took over a tiny cabin that was on the road allowance across the road from the elementary school. We lived as squatters on that land. Initially it was one room with a packed mud floor. We all slept in a row on the mud floor on blankets (Dad later put in a wood floor). No mattresses. There was a stove in the middle of the room for heat and cooking. In winter when it was 40 below zero, someone would have to get up in the middle of the night and stoke the stove. We had no inside toilet and no running water. We didn't even have electricity or a telephone. We pretty much lived in the bush. Uncle Angus was the only one who had a phone in all of the families. He was the only one who had electricity. We didn't get electricity until much later in the game. Dad wired the house himself. I must have been ten years old so that was in the early '60s. Dad was a commercial ice-fisher in winter and worked on the farms in the summer.

Poverty has an ugly face. I was scarred by it, we all were. We knew we were poor. We were kind of a spectacle in the community for our chronic poverty. Mom's younger sister Ida was an Oblate nun in St. Boniface and would send clothing to us on the train that stopped in nearby Ste. Rose du Lac. We would unload the boxes before tearing through them trying to find something we could wear. These were all hand-me-downs the nuns collected and we would then hand them down between us as we grew out of them. Imagine starting school in the clothes your older brother wore the previous year. That was our reality. I remember a pair of women's shoes in one of those boxes. I got stuck with them. I was laughed at for wearing them but I needed shoes and this was all there was. Kids can be cruel.

Our whole life was based around the monthly grocery bill at the local grocery store owned by the Johnsons. It never got paid off completely but Dad would pay it down whenever he could, enough for us to get credit for the next time. We were all aware of that bill. It was like that Tennessee Ernie Ford song "Sixteen Tons": "I owe my soul to the company store."

I remember one time walking 1½ miles to the grocery store with my dad. I was pulling a cart along the gravel road. He intended to fill the cart with groceries. In the store I was drooling over all the food as I was always hungry back then. Dad loaded up the cart and went up to the counter. He put all the groceries on the counter. Other people were there watching him do this. Mrs. Johnson was standing there waiting to be paid. Dad was expecting to have it all put on our account. She looked at the all the stuff and then at him and said, "You can't put anything more on the bill." We left everything on the counter and walked out. It was a horrible public humiliation and hard for me to see my father, who I admired so much, having to face that. I never forgot it. He was a proud man who came from a proud heritage, a direct descendant of the Renville Rangers of Minnesota. My brother Wally remembers a similar incident, but in that case, Mr. Johnson told Mrs. Johnson to let Mom take the groceries home. If

he hadn't, we'd go hungry and we often went hungry. Sometimes all
we had to eat was oatmeal that Mom heated up on the stove. I used
to try to snare rabbits to help out with food. We had an old single
shot .22 rifle and when I turned twelve, I was allowed to use it to
hunt. One day while hunting I faced a deer but made the mistake
of looking into its eyes and I couldn't shoot it. I just could not kill
something living.

Dad built onto the house as the family grew, Randall Francis
'Randy' Ranville was born in 1950. Walter David 'Wally' Ranville
made his appearance in 1952. And I was born Errol Sydney Ranville
on August 1, 1953 at the hospital in Ste. Rose Du Lac. The family
was rounded out by Norman Ralph Ranville in 1954, Rene Lionel
Ranville born in 1955, and finally Donna Marie Ranville in 1958.
Donald Clifford 'Don' Ranville was born in 1951. He was our first
cousin, the son of my dad's sister, but lived with Uncle Angus for his
first ten years before my mom and dad adopted him at age twelve.
There we were twelve kids in all. Dad added two main floor rooms
and an upstairs over the years as the family expanded. He was an
excellent carpenter.

Because of the age differences between the siblings, it was almost
like we had two separate families. Valerie, Stirling, Delphine, and
Bryan were like one family because they were so much older than
the rest of us. It was like a family within a family. Gordon was in
the middle between the older siblings and the younger ones. He preferred being on his own, reading and writing. We used to call him
the Mad Scientist because he loved information and once organized
and wrote a chronological treatise using a twenty-four-volume ency-
clopedia that Mom bought from a travelling salesman, on payments.
Then there was Randy, Wally, and me and then Don joined the family.
We were close in age and became inseparable, the four of us, like the
four musketeers.

I am continually asked how my nickname came about. Long
before the C-Weed band, I was known as Seaweed. The original

name of the band was Seaweed & the Weeds. We once got stopped by the RCMP who asked me what the name of the band was, I told him, and he repeated Seaweed underweeds. We got a good laugh but not at the time. My nickname started out as Saw Man when I was still a youngster. My uncle Carl was known as Saw Man because he was skilled with a saw and won many sawing contests. I looked like him so I became Little Saw Man and he was Big Saw Man. It went through a number of variations until it settled on Seaweed. Later, once we formed a band, we put Seaweed & the Weeds on the front bass drum head. Seaweed wouldn't fit onto the back of my jacket so my brother Gordon shortened it to C-Weed. We weren't thinking about marijuana. We didn't even know what that was back then.

As kids, we used to play "War" pretending to be soldiers. We also played Cowboys and Indians except we were the cowboys, the good guys, fighting off the Indians, the bad guys. My siblings recall I was always crying and not easy to play with. I was manipulative and had to have my own way or I would go running to my parents as though one of my brothers had killed me. My dad soon got wise to me, though, and stopped believing I was so hurt. One time I got my ass kicked for crying wolf when there was nothing wrong with me. I had a vivid imagination in setting up our pretend play scenarios. These often took us a long way from our house, but my brothers would follow me. A few times that got us into big trouble, returning home long past dark after being lost for some time playing make-believe in the bush. I was always pushing the envelope and sometimes getting all the brothers into trouble for my so-called heroic antics.

I never liked school and never finished. I attended elementary school in Eddystone, grades 1 to 8, and junior high and high school in Ste. Rose du Lac but I dropped out in grade 10 after we moved to Winnipeg. The elementary school was across the road from our house but we had to take a bus to Ste. Rose du Lac for junior high and high school, half an hour on the bus twice a day. School was a very fearful experience for me because I had so much shame. We all felt shame. Poverty carries so much of a stigma and we bore that. But we still managed to have fun, my brothers and me. We were each other's support network and our undoing as well because we would fight, too. There was a lot of competition between all of us, typical sibling rivalry. Our house was like our sanctuary from the rest of the world. The community could be unwelcoming to us. If something or someone shamed me, I would go back to the house. It was my security.

We were never scooped by the residential schools because we were outside the government's radar, not being registered as Treaty Indians. But somehow Stirling ended up at a residential school. I still don't know how they scooped him up. He was the only one. My mom knew something was wrong with those schools even though she was a staunch Catholic. To her the church was everything. It was tough for her to go against the church and keep her children at home. She saw something, she smelled a rat. It turned out to be a bad experience for Stirling. It left him pretty messed up for years.

After Dad wired the house for electricity, we acquired a second-hand Fleetwood combination radio/record player/black-and-white television set from one of Dad's employers named Walter Talpash from Ste. Rose du Lac. He broke horses for this guy. Dad was a great horseman. We only had one channel, CBC Winnipeg. We would watch that station from the time it began broadcasting at 11am until it signed off with the Indian Chief test pattern screen around midnight. We loved the action shows. Living an isolated existence in Eddystone, the television offered a window to the larger world.

But television also reinforced the reality that we were different. It made me a little reflective because our family wasn't like the families we saw on television, the *Leave It to Beaver* or *Father Knows Best* families. I remember watching a John Wayne movie on TV and there he was fighting off the Indians. I was rooting for John Wayne. He's the hero and I'm hoping he'll survive these guys chasing him on horseback. I didn't identify with the Indians in all their feathers, warpaint, and bows and arrows. Then one day in the playground at elementary school someone called me a dirty useless Indian. I was really puzzled because to me Indians were those guys in feathers chasing John Wayne and harassing the settlers. I didn't identify with them. I didn't look like them and I didn't dress like them. "Why are you calling me an Indian? What does that mean?" That was the earliest recollection I have of encountering racism. Of course, as you grow older you learn things and come to understand who you are and what you are. Many of the white kids in our community weren't allowed to befriend the Indigenous kids. That was perpetuated by the parents, and their parents and grandparents. I believe racism in perpetuity is a sickness that the host, at times, doesn't even know that they have a choice to not be racist.

At school, the nuns used to call Don "Black Boy." Like "Hey Black Boy, come over here." He was a bit darker-skinned than the rest of us. There's no excuse for that kind of thing now but times were different then. Indigenous people face racism and discrimination every day. You just have to keep moving on. On the road with the band we would be refused service in restaurants. We laugh about this stuff now but we didn't realize at the time that it was racism. It was just our reality. We used to tease Craig about being our token white man, after all he toked and he was a white man. There was one time when we stopped in Lloydminster at a beautiful fine-dining restaurant for dinner, our reception felt like one of those situations where we weren't going to be served. Or the scene Bob Seeger sings about in the song "Turn the Page." Sure enough, we waited over an hour for our food. When we went to pay on our way out, we wanted to pay individually and there was a bit of a discrepancy as to who had what when we were trying to figure it out the hostess made the statement "I knew there was going to be a problem when all you ethnics walked in" and Craig lost it and said "blow it out of your asshole lady." He was extremely angry, I had never seen him like that before and I have never ever seen him that angry since.

Dad built an extension above the main part of the house, but we needed stairs. Someone in Dauphin was selling a full staircase so I went with my Dad in his panel truck to Dauphin to pick up the staircase, a journey of some fifty miles. I remember that it seemed like forever to drive to Dauphin. I had never been that far from home. The next day I was in school looking at a big map of Canada. Someone had placed a pushpin into the spot where Eddystone was. I found Dauphin so I could see how far my journey had been from Eddystone. It didn't look that far away yet to me it felt like an endless trip there and back. Around the same time, I remember finding Vancouver on the map, on the west coast of Canada. The distance just seemed insurmountable to me. I felt at that moment that I would never, ever get to Vancouver. I would never travel that far away in my life. It seemed impossible for me, this kid in Eddystone, Manitoba, to travel that far. If it took that long to get to Dauphin how long would it take to get to Vancouver?

Even before we had a television, I remember the first time I heard music on the radio. I don't think I was even going to school yet at that point. We had a plastic Viking radio on the fridge in the kitchen. The kids were not supposed to touch it in case we broke it even though it wasn't working. Wally was always fascinated by electronic gadgets, he still is, taking them apart to see how they work. One day he was fiddling around with the radio and all of a sudden we heard music for the first time. It was a song by country singer Kitty Wells. I don't even remember what the song was called but that moment was an epiphany for me. I was transfixed. We all stopped what we were doing to listen. It was like that moment in *The Shawshank Redemption* movie when Tim Robbins' character plays some classical music over the prison PA system. Suddenly everybody stops what they're doing to listen because they hadn't heard music in so long.

That day changed my life. Until then I felt life was painful, a kind of pain that you hide, that you don't want anyone to know you have. You are ashamed to let on that you're struggling so much with the pain of reality, that something is wrong but you just can't quite figure out what it is and you cry in silence at night when the lights are off. Maybe it is poverty and the fact that you live in such a large family where there is never enough food to go around or that there is never enough wood in the house to keep the fire going and it is cold. Or that it's so difficult to acquire water to wash and cook with a horse and toboggan in the winter when you're three miles from the frozen lake where you pick up ice blocks to bring home and melt in the 45-gallon drum that sits in the living room. Yes, it hurts all the time but you do not say it. Instead, you depend so much on the love you feel from your siblings and parents.

The pain went away that day when we listened to the little plastic radio that my brother Wally fixed and suddenly, we heard music. The pain went away that day, at least temporarily. I was transported to a different place like the make-believe places we created in our war games. It was a serene place, an emotional abeyance where you could feel free from any impending calamity, safe. Since that day, music became my special place. Since that day music has clothed me, fed me, saved me from the world living there in poverty in the bush in Eddystone.

Just recalling that moment is very emotional for me. It's been said that the key problem for Indigenous young people has always been that they cannot envision a future for themselves beyond where they are. No role models and no inspiration. I had no way of knowing at the time that what I was hearing on that plastic radio in Eddystone would become my lifeline, my ticket out of poverty and isolation. I had been inspired. But inspiration alone wasn't going to be enough.

It was my Aunt Adeline who provided us with the means to escape a dead-end future. It was a cheap flat-top acoustic guitar with only five strings. No high E string. It was very difficult to buy strings in those days. The nearest music store was in Dauphin. Didn't matter to us. Five strings were better than none. She didn't give it to any of us in particular. She brought it to our house, handed it to my oldest brother Stirling and told him to share it among the boys. Somehow, she knew that the guitar was going to save our lives, keep us out of jail, and get us out of the cycle of poverty. Needless to say, we all gravitated toward that guitar. Bryan gave it the name Darlene. I don't recall why. Maybe the name was written on the body. Doesn't matter. We fought over Darlene, the six of us brothers, Stirling, Bryan, Gordon, Randy, Wally and me. We watched each other and learned from each other. I think it came with a book of chords. We learned fast together.

My next oldest brother, Wally, was a major influence on me. He's the one who showed me where to put my fingers on the guitar. I remember I signed up for a talent show at our elementary school across the road. I must have been eight years old. I could barely get my hand around Darlene's neck but Wally helped me pick a song and showed me how to play the chords. I got up onstage and performed the song, "Don't Stop the Music" by George Jones, but something surprising and wonderful happened afterwards. People applauded. I had never experienced that before and it solidified in me the desire to be a singer. I later won a talent show in Dauphin that was aired live on CKDM radio. I won second prize, fifteen silver dollars, which was a lot of money back then. This was another one of the special moments that encouraged me to pursue a career in music.

Not long after, our aunt Annette, our dad's sister, brought a second-hand record player to our house in Eddystone while she stayed with us for a time. Along with the player, she brought some records, country stuff like the Carter Family, Hank Snow and Jimmy Rodgers. That's pretty much the only type of music we heard to that point so we learned it on the guitar. Then, in early 1964, Bryan bought a Beatles 45 in Dauphin and brought it home. It was "Love Me Do," the Fab Four's debut single. We had no way of knowing who The Beatles were or their international fame, isolated as we were. On first listen, I could tell that this music and this band were different. We played it over and over, entranced by what, to us, was an exotic sound, the sound of rock 'n' roll. It was angelic. I still get goosebumps hearing that song and recalling that moment today. Music has the power to transport you from your reality. Then we heard "She Loves You" and it blew our minds. Like a million other kids across North America, we wanted to be The Beatles. So, the four of us became a band. We became the Beatles: Randy, who was really the instigator of all this, on guitar was John Lennon; Wally, also on guitar (we didn't know what a bass was at that time nor could we have afforded one anyway), was Paul McCartney; Don was George Harrison, although Don would later take on drum duties as I moved up to sing. I was the youngest of the four and wanting just to fit in. I became the most unpopular Beatle, Ringo Starr, but at least I was in the band. We had a focus and a purpose. Nothing was more important in our lives than being a band and playing rock 'n' roll. It was then that we became Seaweed & the Weeds.

We did not worry about hunger, no shoes to wear to school, the inherent suffering that comes with not having any money, not having any opportunity of any kind. All of that stuff wasn't important anymore, the band was the most important part of our lives. Music was our lives.

Of course, the odds of a bunch of Beatle-crazed Indians from the bush in Manitoba ever making it in the music business were beyond daunting. This was virtually non-existent. But I never gave it a second thought. I was single-minded in my goal to make music my life. The Beatles never knew just how far their influence spread.

Country music was pretty much all we heard until later when we tuned into Winnipeg rock and roll stations. Elvis, Bill Haley, Chuck Berry, Buddy Holly, the Beach Boys? We missed all of them. Our introduction to rock 'n' roll came via The Beatles. We were now able to pick up a rock 'n' roll radio station, CKY from Winnipeg, so we had a lot of catching up to do. And our repertoire expanded exponentially.

The extent of our Beatles obsession is best illustrated by our acquisition of their December 1965 album *Rubber Soul*. Where kids in Winnipeg could hop on a downtown bus and purchase the new album at Eaton's, The Bay or any of the innumerable record stores along

Portage Avenue, we didn't have that luxury. When we heard about a new Beatles album, I'm guessing from a schoolmate in the community, Wally, Don, Randy and I hitchhiked all the way to Winnipeg in winter to buy the album. We purchased it at Music City near the bus depot, then hitchhiked home clutching our new prized possession in our cold hands.

Stirling was a good guitar player and singer, probably the best singer among us boys. But he loved country music, notably Merle Haggard, so C-Weed & the Weeds, as we had now become, wasn't his thing. He and my cousin Steve made a recording at Dauphin Musical Supply and pressed it into a 45 but I hadn't got that far yet. Stirling, however, would go on to play a big role in the evolution of the band a few years later. He also pioneered the country music bar scene on Winnipeg's Main Street referred to as "the strip."

Everyone would tell me to go sing in the outhouse. My voice hadn't changed yet and I took a lot of flak in those early days. Actually, you could get a pretty good sound in there so once we started up the band, we would practise singing in the outhouse so we could hear the voices blending. But Mom and Dad were very good about letting us rehearse in the house.

Gradually we began to acquire more instruments. Randy bought his guitar, a Canora electric solid-body, from Johnson's General Store in Eddystone, on the bill. Don ordered a $69.99 Saturn semi-hollow body electric guitar from the Eaton's catalogue. It looked like a George Harrison-style guitar. He was still living with Uncle Angus so when Angus heard about that purchase, he hit the ceiling. That was a lot of money back then. Don was in the doghouse for a while. Either Bryan or Stirling had purchased a little Symphonic amplifier for the guitars.

We used to ogle the instruments and equipment in the Eaton's catalogue. They had a limited selection, but it was dreamland for us. For the longest time we didn't see any microphones in the catalogue but finally we spotted a little brown plastic microphone. It looked like

Errol (top) and Randy and Wally (bottom)

one those microphones from the Grand Ole Opry in the 1950s. It was $14.95. We struggled to get that money to order it because it would come to the post office COD. They would send it right back if we didn't have the money when it arrived at the post office. No adding it to our bill. So, when it came in, of course we didn't have enough money. The postmaster threatened to send it back three times. We kept asking him to just hold off a little longer. We'll get the money. We were two or three dollars short. Finally, one of our uncles came through for us and gave us the remainder of the money. Now I could sing with the band and be heard. Before that it was just acoustic singing without a microphone. We bought a little snare drum that had a little gadget that came out from underneath the stand that held a tiny cymbal. It looked like a cactus, the snare drum and the cymbal sticking out and up. But it was a drum to keep the beat. Man, we were rocking.

In the summer months we would dig Seneca roots, dig them up with shovels, slaving away from dawn until dusk in the bush around Eddystone. We would sell them to Johnson's general store. I think we earned about fifteen cents a pound. With the money we saved up we bought a piggyback Kent amplifier from Dauphin Musical Supplies. It had a ten-inch speaker and cost $120. We could plug one guitar and my plastic microphone into it. We called it our PA. We were very proud of that piggyback amp. It looked so professional. This was the beginning of our sound, however meager it was.

We rehearsed diligently. Our friends would come around to watch. We didn't have a bass guitar so Wally played rhythm guitar on the bass setting so it had some bottom to it. Later he began tuning down the bottom two strings to sound like a bass guitar.

We received a lot of support and encouragement for our musical endeavours from our older brothers. Bryan was working for the federal government in Winnipeg by then and he bought us a speaker column and a Bogen metal amplifier for a PA system. We could run a guitar and microphone into that and use the piggyback amp for another guitar. Gordon went to work for Manitoba Highways in Winnipeg. With his first paycheque, he bought us a full drum kit and sent it to us on the Greyhound bus to Ste. Rose du Lac because the bus did not come all the way into Eddystone. We dragged all these boxes into the house and unpacked them. But we didn't know how to set them up. Finally, we figured it out. Wally and Randy had learned to play The Ventures instrumental song "Walk Don't Run." It was one those songs everybody played back then. They started playing "Walk Don't Run" and Don sat down at the kit. When the stop came in the song where the drums do a fill, Don played it and nailed it. We were stunned. They played the song six times in a row that night. Don became our drummer.

C-Weed & the Weeds—Randy, Wally, Don and me—became popular in and around our community. It didn't matter that we were Indigenous, as the music transcended the racism: It was all about the music. We played the popular songs of the day like "Little Red Riding Hood." Everyone really liked us. If people got together for a party they'd say "Go get the Ranvilles" and we would come over and perform. Sometimes we would be woken up in the night to come down to wherever they were partying and we'd play. The old Rancher's Dance Hall in Eddystone would be packed and we would play. There were no liquor licenses in those days, so people would come in and they would have lots of beer sitting on the floor beside their chairs. We even played on the Ebb and Flow reserve. The Chief had a fantastic PA system so we enjoyed playing there.

At that point, we had been playing for Indigenous audiences, kids and adults. We made our very first public appearance to a mixed audience in the summer of 1965 at the community Hall in the town of Laurier a few miles south west of Eddystone. I was twelve years old. We organized the dance, charging $.50 per head. We had to pay for the dance hall but the rest of the money was ours. At the end of the night, we had made $82. I could not believe it. We brought that money home, it was all in $1 bills and coins, and dumped it all out on the kitchen table in our little shack in the bush in Eddystone. None of us had ever seen that much money before. We were all just kind of sitting around staring at it. And I was thinking, this is how I am going to make my living.

After that we started playing dances everywhere in the neighbouring communities. The Christmas dance, the Sadie Hawkins dance, New Year's Eve dance, anything related to Ste. Rose du Lac high school because that's where we were attending school. All I wanted to do was play music. I didn't care about school, or, more precisely I cared even less than I had about school. It wasn't that my parents wanted us to quit school. They wanted us all to graduate from high school. It's that we convinced them that music was the only thing we wanted to do. We were so passionate about the band. It was more important than anything else for us as teenagers. The writing was on the wall and our parents recognized that we weren't going to do anything else.

I remember a Christmas party we played at our house. Uncle Angus was there. Don asking him what he thought of the band. Angus replied, "Well boys, it sure sounds good when you stop." I loved that guy.

It was obvious that we had a measure of talent, potential and plenty of determination. What we didn't have was the means to take those qualities further, out of the bush and the Indigenous house parties to a wider audience. There were no opportunities for us living in Eddystone. Did I want to become an itinerant laborer like my dad, living from paycheque to paycheque? Gradually our parents came to the same conclusion. If we were ever to have a shot at our dream, it would have to be from a larger place, Winnipeg. But there were also plenty of temptations in the big city: alcohol, drugs and crime. I remember them talking to us about that. They worried about the negative side of life in the city. But if we stayed in Eddystone, there was no future for us. It was huge gamble for all of us but, in the end, they decided to pull up what little stakes we had and move the family to Winnipeg. Mom and Dad so loved their children that they made that ultimate and fateful sacrifice knowing that our dreams could never be fulfilled in Eddystone.

Everything we had there in Eddystone is now gone. Our house is gone; it burned down. Dad and Mom and some of my siblings are buried in the church cemetery along with my beloved wife, Marcie. My cousins from my mother's side are very diligent in the upkeep of the cemetery. Other than that, there is little left that connects me to that place anymore. Just mixed feelings and bittersweet memories.

CHAPTER 2

Play Me My Favourite Song

I was always drawn back to the Main Street Strip because that was where I was appreciated. It was definitely the only place I could go where I felt safe and relaxed among our own people. Aboriginal artists were not welcome in other venues that weren't Aboriginal. We didn't pursue white venues because we knew we'd have the door slammed in our faces. It would have been great to play for white people but we didn't get to. We were very proud of who we were.—*Billy Joe Green, musician*

The C-Weed band faced the kind of racism that Indigenous musicians as a whole had to deal with. Unless you're Indigenous, you don't know how bad it was. It was like the Deep South, club manager comes out, sees the band is Indigenous and says, "You guys can't play here." That was the reality. It was kind of like Apartheid. But the C-Weed Band members both individually and collectively earned the respect of other non-Indigenous musicians and that went a long way in their eventual success. It was like, "Wow, you guys grew up in the bush and you can play like that?!" In spite of the racism they faced in the business, they enjoyed the camaraderie and acceptance of other musicians beyond their own community. They were respected by their fellow musicians. But I think a big factor as well was family. They were all family members and family is the best support system you can have.—*David McLeod, Executive Director NCI (Native Communications Incorporated)*

We had already made a couple of forays into Winnipeg in 1966-67 to play the Indian & Métis Friendship Centre at 73 Princess Street in the Exchange District. The Feathermen were like the house band there. They had been around for a while and even played a reception for Prime Minister Pierre Trudeau. They billed themselves as an "All Indian Band," a bold statement to make at a time when being an Indigenous musician was hardly much of a calling card. But they were very proud of who they were. The Feathermen were on a whole other level than us. Percy and Martin Tuesday (along with Chuck Scribe, Morris McArthur, and Angus Monroe) had been in the band and Billy Joe Green had just joined. These guys would go on to become legends on the Indigenous music scene. They had professional instruments and amplifiers, Fender Telecaster guitars and Vox amps, compared to our cheap gear. And they were all grownups. We looked like kids to them, and we were, but they took a liking to us and called us up to jam a few times. The Feathermen were a cover band. So were we when we started out, but once I began writing songs, that set us apart from all the other bands. We surpassed them because we developed our own sound and wrote and recorded our own songs. Nonetheless, as NCI's Dave McLeod noted, "The Feathermen brought Native soul to rock 'n' roll and were real groundbreakers."

Indigenous teens at the Friendship Centre wanted rock 'n' roll and that was our stock in trade so we went over very well. I think that may have been the turning point for my parents, seeing that there might be places for us to play in Winnipeg and that we could earn some money through playing music.

They moved the whole family that was still living in Eddystone, lock, stock and barrel, in late December 1968. I was fifteen, soon to be sixteen. I had a friend who loaned us a 1959 Dodge station wagon. We packed all that we could pack and loaded the rest—dishes, the silverware, towels, blankets—into a box on a roof rack. We had no mattresses, no fridge, no stove. My niece, Roxanne Shuttleworth, said we looked like the Beverly Hillbillies heading off to Los Angeles. Bryan was already in Winnipeg and he was our point man, reconnoitering for a suitable house. He found one at 464 Bannerman Street between Andrews and Powers in Winnipeg's tough North End for $400 a month. Social Services helped out with the rent.

It was a respectable-looking two-storey house, likely built around the 1920s, with three bedrooms upstairs and a basement. But we all slept in a row on the floor on blankets until we started getting beds, one or two at a time. And I remember all my mom had to cook on was an electric frying pan. She would pour macaroni into it then mix in Hamburger Helper and ground beef, filling it right up to the top. It was almost leaking over. We ate in shifts. Once one group had been served, she would mix up another batch for the next ones. She would do this three times for dinner. That way everyone in the house was able to eat. And that is how we started our first few months in Winnipeg, without a fridge and stove. Eventually we bought an old beat-up fridge at a second-hand store, later on a stove, all mismatched. But despite the spartan living conditions there was plenty of love and laughter and partying.

I was in grade 10 when we moved to Winnipeg. I enrolled at St. John's High School in January 1969. Oh man, talk about intimidation coming from rural Ste. Rose du Lac high school. St. John's High: gigantic with three floors. I used to get lost in there because there were doors on all four sides of the building. I didn't know which door to use or what street I came out on. And I did not have any glasses. I could not see very well. I was too scared to sit in the front of the class because I was the new kid and didn't want to draw any further attention. So, I would always sit right at the back. As a result, I couldn't see what was going on in front or on the chalkboard. I ended up quitting. I went home and was scared to tell my mom. She started to cry. My parents had wanted us to finish school. She replied, "Well, if you are going to quit school, then you will have to get a job."

The younger boys, including me, took construction jobs. I began working as a bricklayer's helper but I wasn't very strong and the work was quite backbreaking. We all brought our paycheques home and put the money on the table for the family. C-Weed & the Weeds continued to play the Indian & Métis Friendship Centre. Girls started taking notice of us there. One time we had about thirty girls follow us back to our house after a Friendship Centre gig and Mom flipped out and chased them out of the house. We tried to get booked in other venues around the city. I remember getting into a car and driving to a bunch of pubs to get them to book us but we were met with the same answer at each stop. "We don't want your kind." It wasn't about the music; it was about the audience we attracted: Indians. They were scared of Indigenous people.

Stirling landed a gig at the Brunswick Hotel beverage room on the Main Street Strip north of Portage and Main. The drinking age was still twenty-one. He was old enough, but he brought along Wally (who now owned a bass guitar) and Don to back him up and they were under age. Don used to wear baggy pants because he thought it made him look older (it didn't, he just looked ridiculous). Wally grew a mustache. They called themselves alternately The Ranville Brothers, Ranville Incorporated or Stirling Ranville and the Ranville Trio. Willie Nepinak played with them for a time and later Al Shorting. There weren't a lot of bands playing in bars and pubs in 1969, and there certainly weren't any Indigenous bands in the pubs so they were trailblazers.

Winnipeg in 1969 was alive with music. The live music scene still centered around the many neighbourhood community clubs that hosted dances every weekend. Schools were another source of gigs. And the social, a Manitoba tradition of holding a fundraising party/dance for a soon-to-be-wed couple or for just about any cause, offered fun gigs. There were local record labels releasing locally-produced records. The Guess Who, featuring Randy Bachman and Burton Cummings, were the local kingpins, soon to conquer the world beginning with "These Eyes" in May 1969 and followed by a half-dozen gold and platinum records on the *Billboard* music charts. Neil Young had emerged from the Winnipeg music scene and by 1969 had become a major force in music as both a solo artist and member of Crosby, Stills, Nash & Young. The Fifth, Sugar 'n' Spice, and Mongrels were top draws on the local teen dance circuit. Young As You Are on CJAY TV featured local performers each week, hosted by singer Joey Gregorash. The drinking age would lower to 18 in September 1970 and open up the pubs to rock bands. On the country music circuit Ray St. Germain, Art Young, and Eddie Laham were popular.

However, when you look back at the thriving rock music scene in and around Winnipeg in the 1960s and '70s, it was almost exclusively white. There were few visible minorities represented and of those even fewer Indigenous musicians. Indigenous musicians gravitated to the Main Street Strip and the many hotel beverage rooms located along Main Street North between McDermot Avenue, past the CPR Main Street underpass, up to Euclid Avenue. Establishments such as the Woodbine, Bell, Occidental, and Yale hotels, among others, hired Indigenous performers. You were playing for your own people and they appreciated you. Farther west on Keewatin Street were the Westbrook (formerly the Waldorf) and Brooklands hotels which also featured Indigenous talent. But the hot spot was the Brunswick Hotel at 571 Main Street (now a parking lot north of the Manitoba Museum). All these venues required bands to play a three-hour set every afternoon, 3:00 to 6:00 then an evening set from 9:00 to midnight, later extended to 1:00 am. It was grueling work and the pay was horrendous: $8 per player for the afternoons and $8 for the evening. If you complained you were fired. The owner also threatened that if you played any of the other hotels on the strip you were done at the Brunswick. You would never play there again.

The Brunswick hadn't featured live music before Stirling approached the owner. He agreed to hire the Ranvilles and had a tiny stage built in one corner of the pub. I was too young to be in the band so I was locked out of that scene. Instead, when I was seventeen I joined the travelling midway at the Morris Stampede and travelled with the Gayland Shows all the way to Prince George, BC where we were let go and the show moved on into the USA. While we were making our way to Prince George, the last stop of the carnival circuit, the driver jackknifed the truck I was travelling in and took off, leaving us stranded in North Battleford, SK. It was August 1st, my eighteenth birthday, so I called home collect and spoke with mom for a while. I spent the rest of my birthday lying under the truck in my sleeping bag trying to stay out of the rain. I was travelling with my friends the Roussin brothers; when we got on the train in Prince George, BC to head home to Winnipeg, we were stoned on acid and had no money for food or drinks all three days of our journey home. I remember coming down in a railway station switching trains in Edmonton and trying to sleep on a bench and a baby started crying a few seats behind me. That was such a mournful sound when you're coming down. I arrived at the train station in Winnipeg and walked down Main Street towards the Brunswick Hotel where my brothers were with my empty guitar case because my guitar had been stolen in Prince George. I arrived at the Brunswick just as the boys were ready to play on Friday afternoon at 3 o'clock. Oh man, I wanted to join the band so badly. I borrowed my brother Bryan's identification and would get in as Gerald Bryan Ranville. Stirling would let me up to sing a few songs from time to time and the place would go crazy because I would sing rock songs, Credence Clearwater songs like "Who'll Stop the Rain," "Have You Ever Seen the Rain," Cream,

Eric Clapton, "Gloria." These songs got the crowd up and happening. Gradually I sang more often. Randy had dropped out after we moved to Winnipeg. He had a steady job and a girlfriend, soon to be his wife, and preferred a more stable life. Stirling began having problems with alcohol and eventually had to bow out. He spent some time in hospital so I became the singer at the Brunswick and it was C-Weed & the Weeds—me, Wally and Don—once again.

During the time we held court at the Brunswick Hotel, the beverage room led the province in beer sales. Slowly other hotels not on Main Street or Keewatin began taking a chance on Indigenous musicians. The Balmoral later booked us, as did the Airport hotel.

Before Stirling left the Brunswick and the band, he set up bank accounts for the band and its members. He sought to run the band like a business. He wanted the band members to take music seriously as a business and try to make a living from it. He was far-sighted in that. I learned a lot from him about how to put a band on a solid financial footing and run it as a business. Stirling taught me that.

If Eddystone was the start of what would become C-Weed, then the Brunswick was the next step. We held court there for three years in the early 1970s. We played seven hours a day, six days a week. Social scientist Malcolm Gladwell in his 2011 book *Outliers: The Story of Success* talks about the 10,000-hour rule which states that if someone puts in 10,000 hours of practice at something, they will be an expert in whatever that something is. Consider the case of The Beatles, who played hundreds of hours in Hamburg, Germany's gritty nightclubs. By the time they returned to Liverpool they were a much better, tighter band than before they left. Fans and pundits alike noticed the difference. Now, I'm not about to compare our band to The Beatles, I'm just making the point that the more playing you do, or the more practice you have, the odds are you're going to be much better at what you do. And that was the case with C-Weed. The Brunswick hotel was our Hamburg, our crucible. Music was our church and the Brunswick beverage room was where we worshipped.

That was quite a rush. Putting it in perspective, we came from chronic poverty and a kind of survival mode to anchoring the Brunswick Hotel, of all places. It may not have been much money, but it was a steady gig and a steady living. We knew we wouldn't be there forever.

Wally, Don and I had the magic together. We grew up together and we grew together. We shared the same dreams. Wally and Don are my support system. No matter what the emotional baggage might be going on between us, the band and the music trumped it all. The show must go on, and we always knew that. We all needed that applause. People came to see the Ranville Brothers playing together, and they still do.

It was during this period of steady work at the Brunswick that I became this alter ego, C-Weed. There was no such thing as Errol in those days. A lot of people did not even know my real name. So, of course, it gave me an edge, so to speak. C-Weed was born there. And it kind of scared me a little bit, too. I had to sort of take in this phenomenon and come to terms with it slowly and I think I suffered the consequences of it happening too fast at certain stages. More about that later. Gradually I became C-Weed and C-Weed became the name of the band. It did cause some resentment in our all-for-one-and-one-for-all ethos but it was the way the public came to perceive me and the band.

We never regarded ourselves as the greatest musicians. However, together we were tight and sounded good. We were headstrong, passionate, dedicated and motivated but when veteran Indigenous guitarist Jimmy Flett joined us, that really elevated our stature. Originally from the Ebb and Flow reserve, Jimmy was our cousin and one of the finest musicians on the Winnipeg Indigenous music scene. He was a guitar virtuoso who played circles around just about everyone on the local scene at the time. Jimmy was older and already well known when he joined us. When he was added to the mix that was a big deal for us. We were in awe of him. We couldn't believe that a guy of Jimmy Flett's caliber would join us, three kids from the bush. He lifted all of us up, collectively and individually. Jimmy validated us and gave us confidence as a band. With Jimmy, we thought we were the best band in the world. Even though he didn't go the distance with us, we would not have gotten to where we were without Jimmy Flett.

The most successful musicians and bands are the ones who realize early on that the key to success lies in writing your own songs. You need your own songs, your own voice, your own statement. I recognized that fact when I was twelve years old. That's when I started writing. I was a shy kid so when I began to write songs, I couldn't share them with anyone, not even my brothers. I was too self-conscious. Finally, when I was fourteen, I showed Wally one of my songs. He listened quietly, intently, paused for what to me seemed like forever, then finally said, "You got any more?" That was my validation. He made me sing them all into my sister Delphine's little cassette tape player. Everything I had written to that point. Then I lost the tape.

Bryan was a big fan of Canadian-born folksinger/songwriter Buffy Sainte-Marie and he brought one of her records home when we were still in Eddystone. I wasn't into her music. We were rock 'n' rollers and she was a bit old for our tastes. Nonetheless, I listened to her song "Take My Hand For Awhile." I played it over and over again, taking in the lyrics and the story she was telling. That song touched me in a way no other song had done. It was a haunting love song and it made me cry. I remember thinking that I didn't have any choice in the matter, that the song just took me somewhere else emotionally. That's the point when I realized I wanted to do that, to be able to touch people with my music. I wanted to write a song that could affect people in that same way.

I wasn't much of a book reader as a kid (I'm a voracious novel reader now). So where do my songs come from? I've been asked this question throughout my career. I remember seeing an interview on TV with country music singer/songwriter Merle Haggard after he won a Country Music Award for his song-writing. He was asked what it was that helped him write so many great songs. His reply stunned me. "I believe all songs are already written and a chosen few of us get to hear them and write them down," he stated. The hair on the back of my neck stood up when I heard him say that. I had thought I was the only one who experienced that. I understood implicitly what Merle was saying but I would never tell anybody because I feared they would think I was losing my mind. I hear a song, it comes to me, and I've got to get it written down before I lose it. I've lost more songs than I've recorded simply by not catching them when they were passing by. They only come by once. Now I keep my phone by my bed so that when the muse hits, I can record it before it's lost forever. I just sing what I hear into my phone and if there is a guitar riff I hum that too.

While opportunities remained limited for Indigenous musicians in Winnipeg, that was not the case outside city limits. Reserves and rural communities with Indigenous populations were starving for live music from their own people. There was an entire untapped market just waiting for Indigenous performers. Chief Walter Monias of the Cross Lake Reserve north of the top of Lake Winnipeg came to the Brunswick one night and witnessed the continuous lineup at the door and sometimes right down the street, people wanting to see an all-Indigenous band playing for Indigenous audiences. The Ranville Trio was performing. Chief Monias apprehensively approached Stirling and inquired if we would consider coming up to his community to perform. Stirling was bold enough to accept. The band drove to Wabowden in our old beat-up vehicles. There was no highway yet. The number 6 highway was a dirt trail filled with ruts. We chartered an airplane from Wabowden to get us to Cross Lake. We were welcomed warmly and they paid enough to make the trip worthwhile. That got the ball rolling. The Ranville Trio began travelling to isolated reserves to entertain the people who were not able to travel out to Winnipeg to see us play live at the Brunswick hotel. Nobody else was doing it; we invented a new circuit for Indigenous bands to play outside of Winnipeg.

This is where my brother Bryan stepped in. He was like our very own Brian Epstein, manager of the Beatles. If it wasn't for Bryan there would be no C-Weed Band. Bryan had always supported us in whatever way he could after he left Eddystone. He bought us equipment and provided us with a lot of encouragement. He took a job with the federal government in the Secretary of State department in Toronto before settling in Ottawa. Situated in the center of government services, Bryan became our spin doctor. He knew how to work the media. And more importantly, he had connections and the inside track with all the reserves across the country. He knew the chiefs and, more significantly, when federal money was going out to all the reserves. He used this information to promote the C-Weed Band to reserves. We had been playing the Brunswick Hotel for several years now and were looking for better opportunities. Bryan became the catalyst for the next step in our career. We left the Main Street Strip and headed out on the wide-open road. When we vacated our spot at the Brunswick, Billy Joe Green and his band moved in and held a residence there for several years.

Playing northern reserves was often arduous. I remember driving all the way up to Wabowden where we would board a small Beaver bush plane with holes in the floor and the old round radial engines that sputtered and died every once in a while and had to be restarted. We flew into Cross Lake since there was no road in there yet. We drove over the Number 6 highway from Lake St. Martin to Ponton which was still a dirt trail, not even a gravel grade. We would have to take a 45-gallon barrel of fuel with us as we did not have enough fuel to run the old van from Lake St. Martin to Grand Rapids which was the next fuel stop. Everybody else was staying safe in their homes in Winnipeg while we were out there breaking trail in the minus 40 degree winters with old beat-up vehicles. It is a wonder we didn't freeze to death on the highway one of those nights with a breakdown. We had some close calls, but we pushed on into territories where no bands had played yet.

I don't know if anybody realized it at the time, but by shutting us out of the big clubs in Winnipeg, the 'White' rooms, it forced us out on the road. That was the best thing for us. And when we got on the road, we packed every place we played. We had a hell of a good time. We soon bought an old bus, refurbished it for travel, and just ended up living in it.

On May 19, 1975, we performed at Winnipeg's plush 2,400-seat Centennial Concert Hall for a show billed as the Manitoba Métis Federation Country Jam. It sold out. Len Fairchuck was hosting *The Western Hour* at that time, a popular weekly Indigenous country music show on CKND television. I thought that if we brought the quality up a little bit, our show might be more appealing. Not to knock anything that Len Fairchuck was doing—he is a legend to Indigenous people and referred to with reverence as White Buffalo—we just hoped that we could possibly do something bigger and better at a bigger venue. That was a major coup for us. I produced the show and performed with the C-Weed Band. We had a huge C-Weed neon sign and raised it at the back of the concert hall stage. We ordered the sign from Belle Fosh Signs on McDermot Avenue and they wanted $800 for it. We couldn't imagine paying that kind of money. We offered to use the sign for the show then bring it back but they weren't going to make it just to have it returned. However, they were good enough to let us take it and pay it off when we could. We were able to pay a little bit at a time. We took that nice blue neon sign and hoisted it up behind the band at the Concert Hall. People were blown away. We felt like stars. That was the first time we started branding the name C-Weed. We carried that sign all over the country after that. It ended up burning in the fire when my C-Weed's Cabaret club was torched in Edmonton, Alberta by drug dealers that I had barred out.

The Concert Hall was on the next block south of the Brunswick Hotel on Main Street but it couldn't have been more polar opposite, light years away. It was a multi-act variety show, all Indigenous artists, including Gloria and Lionel Desjarlais; the Dutiaume Brothers, Clint and Tom, who were just kids; the C-Weed Band; and Ray St. Germain. What a learning curve for me. I remember coming out on that stage that night just in a panic. I could barely breathe and thought I was going to faint. But once I got through the first thirty seconds and saw that I was still standing, it went well from there. The sound of applause coming from a Concert Hall full house is a moment I won't soon forget. Definitely a highlight in my career. We went on to play shows in larger and more elegant venues after that, including Winnipeg's venerable Playhouse/Pantages Theatre, but that first Concert Hall show ranks right up near the top for me.

The entire Concert Hall experience was wonderful. I booked the hall myself, printed the tickets, made the posters, and sold the tickets, all with my fingers crossed that this expensive and risky endeavor would work. I wasn't looking to make money, just to break even. Even the dressing rooms behind the stage area was exciting. We'd never had dressing rooms before.

The sound of the band was evolving from Top 40 rock 'n' roll to country rock, or outlaw or rebel rock as it was often called. The Eagles opened that door and country rock was happening. We started out playing a lot of Merle Haggard and Willie Nelson songs when we first played the Brunswick because that's what Stirling had been doing. Gradually, we began adding Leonard Skynyrd and Pink Floyd songs. Once we started playing reserves, we saw whole families coming out to our shows. We tried to offer the entire gamut from fiddle songs to traditional country to country rock. And in doing so we invented our sound, the C-Weed sound.

I had an attitude, we all did. We were Canadian music outlaws, a band of Indian brothers who didn't conform. We stopped wearing matching band outfits like most other bands continued to do. We wore whatever we wanted because it was about the music and in that we were deadly tight. We came to be regarded by the Canadian music business as unmanageable because of our attitude and the racism in the music scene. We were a band of Indians who didn't do what others told us to do. Plus being brothers, we were more close-knit, than other bands.

Having learned to play on the cheapest instruments and equipment, now we became equipment junkies. We pooled our money to buy more and better gear. Sound was important to us. We didn't like using a house PA system because it might be inferior and jeopardize our sound so we started travelling with our own PA, which meant we would need trucking and we would require our own sound tech to travel with us. Wally trained our cousin Fred Hayes to set up and run the soundboard. Sadly, Fred passed away during the writing of this book. By the beginning of the 1980s, we had a giant PA system we rented from Gerry Leger at Oakwood Audio. It was the envy of our contemporaries. Everywhere we played people were in awe of our sound. None of the other bands around were mixing sound offstage or travelling with roadies. We had begun to set ourselves apart from the pack.

Playing reserves made us aware that people looked up to us. Here we were, a band of Indians, making music and travelling the land, living the life. We were becoming role models for young Indigenous kids who looked up to us and envied us. All of a sudden, we were heroes to people. I had never envisioned that role for myself when I dreamed of being a musician. I didn't want that kind of responsibility and I still don't, but it comes with the territory and you have to accept it. I didn't have a choice in the matter. As far as we were concerned, we were just having fun and partying our asses off.

It's at that moment that I realized we had to clean up our act, meaning how we presented ourselves in public. Whether we liked it or not, Indigenous people, especially young Indigenous people, looked up to us and we had to live up to their expectations of us. We carried their hopes and dreams. I started getting on the other guys about how we acted. Sure, on the bus we drank and smoked dope and all that, but in public we had to act a certain way, responsible and respectable. We couldn't be drunken Indians. Everything we did was under a microscope and we had to be careful. We were living in a fishbowl and everything was scrutinized. This became magnified even more so once we started having hit records in the 1980s. Things like when you leave a hotel, do not take anything that belonged in the room because it would reflect badly not just on us but on Indigenous people as a whole. The other guys in the band bought into it and went along with it. Sure, we still partied, but we didn't pour ourselves off the bus in a drunken stupor. We didn't want that kind of reputation because it would reflect on the broader Indigenous community. We also started screening the hangers-on around us and at gigs. If a white band partied hard it was taken for granted as just embracing the rock 'n' roll lifestyle of sex, drugs and rock 'n' roll. But if we did it, then it made headlines because we were Indians. Of course, there were people around that were just waiting for us to mess up so that they could point their fingers at us and see us fail, which didn't happen. Every hit song on the radio drew us forward to the next successful tour.

CHAPTER 3

Bringing Home the Good Times

"Growing up, it was a big deal for me to have albums by Ernest Monias, Red Wine and C-Weed. These were groundbreaking just in the sense of having their voices, a Native voice, on an actual vinyl record. That was part of the mythology as well, that you could actually play records by Indigenous recording artists. You'd have albums by the Beatles, Rolling Stones and Eagles and there was a C-Weed Band album there in amongst them. In our community, just having their records was as good as having those other artists' albums.
—*David McLeod, Executive Director, NCI (Native Communications Incorporated)*

We received our Juno nominations before there was a separate Aboriginal music Juno category. We weren't labelled an Aboriginal band and we didn't want to be. We were just a band like any other country rock band and we wanted to be accepted on that basis.
—*Wally Ranville*

The Junos now have an Aboriginal Music Award but the reality is that it means we can't compete with non-Aboriginal artists. 'Oh, you're Aboriginal? Well then you go over there in that category'. We don't get to compete with bands like the Sheepdogs because we're labelled Aboriginal and segregated. We never played the race card. We never said, 'Oh, you don't like us because we're Indians?' Never. We didn't think of our music as Indigenous. It was country rock and rock 'n' roll, good rock 'n' roll. It's not Aboriginal rock 'n' roll, it's just rock 'n' roll. We never wanted to be categorized, pigeon-holed or segregated as an Indian band. We overcame the Indian label and just went out and did it.—*Don Ranville*

Everything we did as a band was in incremental steps toward that proverbial next goal. By 1979 we were ready for that next step, recording and releasing a record. We had established ourselves in the Indigenous community in Manitoba and a little beyond. We headlined another Centennial Concert Hall show on January 14, 1979, Winnipeg Local Country Jam '79, a benefit for The Winnipeg Local Sports Fund. Joining us that night were Red Wine featuring Robbie Brass, Midnight Rider, Gloria Jeffrey (Desjarlais), Lawrence 'Teddy Boy' Houle, Gene Bretecher, and Percy Tuesday. All the local heroes.

Now we needed to solidify our reputation with a record that our fans could hear on the radio and buy. But being an Indigenous band playing rockin' country music wasn't an easy sell to record companies. Nobody was knocking on our door to sign us up.

One of our contemporaries on the Winnipeg Indigenous music scene, Métis singer Gloria Desjarlais, originally from St. Laurent, Manitoba, had a well-earned reputation as a powerful singer. Local MCA Records rep Jack Skelly championed Gloria to the label's executives in Toronto, urging them to sign her on the strength of a song she recorded on her own dime. But the executives' response was "No one's going to buy her records except Indians and they don't have any money" and turned her down. In the end Gloria formed her own record label, John Bull Records, and released a half dozen great singles. It was the same rejection for other Indigenous artists.

If we were ever going to make an album, we would have to finance it ourselves. As a result, between 1979 into 1980, we recorded the tracks for *The Finest You Can Buy* over a considerable period of time, track by track, because we paid for the sessions ourselves and we had to wait until we had the money to record the next tracks. The master tapes sat for months at Century 21 recording studio in suburban Winnipeg because John Hildebrand, one of the studio owners and recording engineer, wanted to get his money before releasing them to us. He held our album for ransom. Under the circumstances, I don't blame him.

I think it's important to acknowledge those promoters and concert agents who paid the band a little more money for our gigs so that we could pool that money to pay our recording costs: Phil Gardiner, Steve Jourdain, Arnold Constant, Walter Cook, Gerry Spence, Ernie Blais, Jim McIntyre, and Morris Skatch. Their names are mentioned on the back cover of *The Finest You Can Buy*. Their contributions to The C-Weed Band's humble beginnings are undeniable.

We self-produced that first album. Wally was always interested in our sound and played a significant role in mixing the album tracks along with one of the studio owners, Harry Hildebrand. His brother John Hildebrand served as engineer. The Hildebrands understood us because they were from a band of brothers, also. The Eternals consisted of the Paley and Hildebrand brothers. They could relate to us.

I think one of the reasons we stood out from other bands, both country rock and Indigenous bands, was that we had original material. I wrote songs for us to record. Sure, we covered some songs, but what made us different and set us apart from our contemporaries was the songwriting. I grew as a writer with each album. I only wrote four songs on our first album *The Finest You Can Buy* but with each album I included more original songs. By the third album, *Going The Distance*, I had found my footing as a songwriter. We took the creative process and the recording process very seriously. When you listen to that first album you can hear a lot going on underneath the basic backing track and lead vocals that did not need to be there. The C-Weed sound matured by the *Going the Distance* album because of my writing but also the dedication of my brother Wally mixing the album. Everybody in the local music industry lauded the sound and Wally's work. The body of work on *Going the Distance* and the amount of hits that came from that one project resembles the Band's work and number of hits they had from their first two albums from Big Pink.

We were playing at a bar in Selkirk, Manitoba when *The Last Waltz* movie came out chronicling the farewell performance of The Band. The Band were four Canadians from southern Ontario, and a Southern rebel from Arkansas: drummer/singer, Levon Helm. Before they became The Band, they were called The Hawks, backing rocka-billy rebel Rompin' Ronnie Hawkins on the early 1960s Ontario bar circuit. They were so tight and original as a back-up band that folk music singer/songwriter Bob Dylan tapped them to support him on his controversial 1965-66 world tour where he was booed everywhere for playing electric rock music. After Dylan suffered a motorcycle accident, the Hawks retreated to a large pink house in upstate New York near Woodstock. Here they wrote a body of songs that would alter the course of popular music. Now known simply as The Band, their debut 1968 album *Music From Big Pink* and its follow up a year later titled *The Band* brought popular music back from psychedelic excess to a rootsy, country, gospel Americana music. By 1976 they had been together almost fifteen years and leader Robbie Robertson decided to call it quits.

Anyway, we played the afternoon jam at the Eveline hotel in Selkirk and had several hours before the evening set at 9 P.M. *The Last Waltz* was playing at the theatre in Selkirk. I suggested to the guys that we grab a quick dinner then go see the movie. We could easily make our 9 P.M. set. We loved the movie, but I took particular notice of one song, "Evangeline." Composed by Robbie Robertson who, the world would learn a few years later, was of Mohawk/Jewish descent. So he was one of us. In the movie, bass player Rick Danko along with Levon Helm sang the song with country singer Emmylou Harris. The result was haunting musical genius in its simplicity. I wanted to add it to our repertoire and managed to get the soundtrack to the movie so we could learn it. We started playing that song in our shows and noticed that older people would get up and dance the old-time waltz to it. It became our most requested song wherever we played. Several chiefs told us we should record the song "Evangeline." We were thrilled to have Guess Who bass player Jim Kale lay down the bass on the track for us. That was very generous of Wally to step aside to let Kale sit in.

The album included a song composed by our friend Billy Joe Green entitled "Hard Hearted Woman" which is one of those songs that still sounds current today. We also covered Hank Williams Sr's "Your Cheatin' Heart" and a song written by local country guitarist Al Shorting called "You're So Mean." A country gospel song called "Let's All Go Down to The River" written by Earl Montgomery and Sue Richards was a duet that I sang with Craig Fotheringham's wife Rhonda Hart that became very popular with country music radio programmers. Another ingredient that gave our first album recording a firm footing in the Canadian country music scene.

We were supported on the album tracks by several players of note including fiddler Stan Winistock, pedal steel guitarists Wes Wilson and Ron Halldorson, harmonica player Garry Preston, Danny Pelfrey on alto saxophone and Craig Fotheringham on piano along with his wife Rhonda Hart on backup vocals. Craig would go on to play a significant role in our career, ultimately serving as producer, arranger, co-writer and finally joining The C-Weed Band on the road.

With the album tracks completed we needed a record label to release it. We could put it out on our own label, but we lacked the ability to distribute the album to the various retail outlets and get it to radio stations. North End Winnipeg-based Sunshine Records had already established a presence in the Indigenous community by releasing recordings by several Indigenous artists including fiddler Reg Bouvette, singer Wayne Fehr, and one of Indigenous music's biggest stars, Ernest Monias. The label's owner had a reputation as a bit of a shady character and we heard plenty of stories about the way he operated, but he offered to sign us. Sunshine Records did not cover any recording costs. We recorded the two albums Sunshine released out of our own pockets and pretty much gave them to Sunshine Records. Thus, it was an easy deal for the label. Their costs were minimal.

Horror stories of so-called 'creative accounting' practices are rampant in the music industry but especially so for Indigenous artists. Despite notching up a huge hit right out of the chute with "Evangeline," we never saw a penny in royalties for two albums with Sunshine Records. We would receive these financial statements full of figures that showed we always owed them money. But we were naive when we signed with them. All we wanted was to have a record out. We knew nothing about the music business. By the time we got to recording our third album, *Going The Distance*, we had figured out what was going on. A lot of Indigenous recording artists were ripped off. The worst example is the case of Ernest Monias. He should be independently wealthy from all the record sales he had through the years. And he's just the tip of the iceberg. All these Indigenous artists who didn't know any better paying thousands of dollars to create their master recordings and getting no money from the sales.

I guess I could have taken the label to court, but I don't have much luck with the courts. The owner and I did have a bit of a row that looked like it could have escalated into physicality.

We took the cover photo for *The Finest You Can Buy* at Sunshine Riding Academy (no relation to the record label), located at the corner of Saskatchewan Avenue and Sturgeon Road in west Winnipeg. The photo showed the five of us—me, Don, Wally, Jimmy Flett and Clyde Roulette—on horseback. The foliage around us is supposed to represent weed, marijuana. The title certainly implied weed. The back cover

The album cover for *The Finest You Can Buy*, featuring me,
Don, Wally, Jimmy Flett and Clyde Roulette

included all the musician credits and a note from Canadian country music legend Dick Damron, who we backed up on the road. In the photos I'm wearing my black cowboy hat. We all tried to emulate the southern rock bands who all wore hats so that's when I got the hat and started wearing it. I didn't wear it just onstage; I wore it all the time. That hat became part of my identity, my trademark, and a signature feature in the band's image to this day.

The first single off the album included two songs that I composed, "Willie The Gypsey" [sic] and "Cindy's Song." The first single, Willie the Gypsey, brought us some attention from radio but it was the second single, Robbie Robertson's "Evangeline" backed by my song "Black Jack Willy" that really took off, eventually hitting #1 on the country music charts right across Canada. It is important to note that this was the mainstream RPM magazine top 100 charts for all of Canada, not the Aboriginal music Top 40 chart that we have now. There was no APTN television yet, there was no Aboriginal music radio yet or the Western Association of Radio Broadcasters. We were competing with mainstream country music. Suddenly we were an overnight sensation, if overnight meant ten years slogging it out in the minor leagues or worse. Everyone wanted to book us. With the single riding atop the charts, we were invited to the Canadian Country Music Awards in Edmonton and played the CBC television special presentation of the awards show. It was too late to be nominated, but they had to acknowledge us in some way because of our hit. It helped that the song was written by an already established artist and a Canadian music legend, Robbie Robertson, who was half Mohawk Indian and half Jewish.

Years later I met Robbie Robertson at the Juno Awards in Toronto at the O'Keefe Centre of the Arts. Whenever I was in Toronto, I would go to lunch with Jason Sniderman, whose father Sam started the Sam The Record Man chain first on Toronto's iconic Yonge Street before spreading out to all the major cities across Canada. We sold a lot of records for them. Jason gave me his fourth-row seats for the event. That was quite something to see it all up close. When Celine Dion came out walking through the dry ice fog singing her monster hit "The Power of Love," I was riveted to my seat. Afterwards, at the reception held across the street from the O'Keefe Centre, I spotted Robbie. Now I'm a shy guy and I'm standing up against the wall not comfortable to speak to anyone when Robbie walks in. Of course, everyone is acknowledging him because he's a big international star. I watched him as he moved around the room and as he did so he spotted me. I was there in my black cowboy hat. I didn't expect him to know who I was but, he comes straight over, puts out his hand and says, "You're C-Weed." He told me that when "Evangeline" came out he was working on the movie *Carny*. He then said, "I was hoping to run into you because no matter how much cash you have, when you get a cheque for thirty grand you want to meet the guy responsible for it. Thank you." It was a special moment for me. And at least *he* got paid.

Suddenly it was a different kind of career. That was the big change for us beginning in 1980. We started fielding calls from every major native event in the country as well as requests to appear on television shows from coast to coast to coast. The demand for the band became huge. We were all over the country. Meanwhile Bryan continued to hustle on our behalf. We would have our tour bus in northern Saskatchewan. We would drive to Edmonton, get on an airplane to Whitehorse. From Whitehorse we would fly to Ottawa. Our bus is still in Edmonton. We are in Ottawa. From Ottawa we flew to Québec City and from there we would finally fly back to Edmonton and move on over the mountains. We lived in airports a lot. Usually at ungodly hours of 5 A.M. or 6 A.M. catching taxi cabs from some hotel or motel.

I hooked up with a booking agent out of London, Ontario and she booked us all across Ontario. We played Dryden, Thunder Bay, Sault Ste. Marie, Sudbury, all the way through to the east coast. I remember the first time we played in Moncton, New Brunswick. That was our first show in the Maritimes. Just after we got into Nova Scotia, I realized that the number 1 highway was then called "Evangeline Trail" and several miles further we entered "Evangeline Provincial Park." This was at the time when our song, "Evangeline" was number one on country music radio across Canada. We arrived in Moncton late and the crew was setting up the show while we were taking showers upstairs. When we came down and were walking through the club

Relaxing at Boot Hill in Tombstone, Arizona

towards the stage, we received a standing ovation and we hadn't even played anything yet. I wondered what was going on. When I got onto the stage there was a railing across the front separating the stage from the dance floor, all along the railing were bits of scraps of paper and upon closer inspection I saw that every one of them was a request for "Evangeline" so we opened with the song and the roof came down. One of those "I'll never forget this moment."

We did the Maritimes and then back to play in Vancouver and up to Whitehorse and Yellowknife. We even toured in the American Southwest in Arizona, New Mexico for the Navajo Nation Fair.

I was in the School of Social Work as an adult student at the University of Manitoba when "Evangeline" went to #1. I had gone back to school in the latter 1970s as a mature student. I enrolled at the Winnipeg Centre Project on Dufferin in the North End, which was an off-campus of Brandon University's extension program for teacher training associated with BUNTEP (Brandon University Teacher Education Program). I went there for two years and had accumulated a list of credits. Music at that time was not really fulfilling my full potential. I played at night so I had all day. I felt I could do more than just sit around waiting to play. I had the capacity to accomplish more. The program ended so I transferred to the University of Manitoba and applied for the School of Social Work. I was interviewed by a panel and they were interested in me because I was Indigenous, the only one applying. They accepted me but not all my credits were transferrable, only 30%. It was almost like starting over, but I was okay with that. I was just happy to be accepted.

I remember sitting with one of my professors, Ray Morrow. We became friends. He was curious that there was an Indian in his class. He wanted to know what that was all about. We were talking about sociology and about the whole social strata, stuff that we were learning in class. He said to me, "Errol, for you to get from where you came from to being here sitting in my class is a huge sociological leap, an impossible leap. I don't know what you are doing here, but stick it out. It is very important that you stay."

I was still playing in the band so I would bring my books and study in the corner of the beverage rooms until the next set. By the time I left the University of Manitoba I only needed one full credit course and one half-credit course to graduate. But then opportunity knocked when "Evangeline" went to #1. I left university in my fifth year and got onto the tour bus. I was gone for the next seven years.

Jimmy Flett left the band once we started venturing farther afield. He was drinking pretty heavily and we couldn't have him in the band anymore. He didn't want to tour. He wanted to stay home with his family and play in and around Winnipeg. No pressure and no expectations on him. I respected that completely. Your family comes first. He knew what he wanted and we soldiered on. As for us, Wally, Don and I, we were prepared to be on the road for months. We were living our dream and were willing to pay the price for our music. We were road warriors. All we needed was a gig to go to, a tank of gas to get us there, and someone to play the lead guitar. Nonetheless, Jimmy played on our first album and on our hit single "Evangeline." His playing elevated the tracks. Jimmy passed away in 2018. I loved that guy and his passion for musical perfection.

Clyde Roulette played dobro and slide guitar on the *High And Dry* album. For a time, we had Ben Mayo in the band on pedal steel guitar but by the time we began recording he moved on to other pursuits.

Here's the thing, though. Unless you knew who C-Weed was, few outside of the Indigenous community across the country knew we were an Indigenous band. This was still years before Country Music Television introduced music videos. Radio would play the single without knowing anything about the band. We were breaking down barriers that kept us out of white markets without even knowing it. But we still had to deal with club owners panicking when they saw us pull up.

We were booked at a club in Edmonton, Alberta called the Cook County Saloon. There are a lot of reserves in the general vicinity of Edmonton. The club owner, Barry Sparrow, knew that there was a band named C-Weed who had a #1 record out. That's why he booked us; we were the hottest recording artists on the charts. That's all he knew. "Get me the #1 country band." We arrived on Sunday afternoon to unload and set up and as we walked in, he realized that we were Indians. He showed us all into the club and then all the boys went back to start unloading the bus and the truck, I detoured into the other side of the stage to inspect the room, I don't think Barry knew I was there when he said to the maintenance man, "These guys are a bunch of Indians!" But on Monday there were so many Indigenous people in line-up to get in that the usual white cowboy crowd couldn't get in. The Indigenous people never went to this bar previously but came out to see us because they wanted to support the band. The manager later told me that he was scared when he saw us arrive and didn't know what was going to happen. He said that after every weekend when there was a packed house, he would have to spend thousands of dollars repairing the washrooms because the white crowds got so rowdy that they punched holes in the walls, pulled off the toilet seats, and smashed the sinks. But when we played there that week, even though there was a packed full crowd every night, there was no damage done. By Thursday night Barry realized the crowd respected the band too much to break anything or do anything to compromise The C-Weed Band name. Saturday night was the biggest night that they had ever had, we held the record there for over two years. Barry and I became good friends and the C-Weed Band played the Cook County Saloon many times.

Another engagement remains memorable for a different reason. We were booked to perform a free show at Edmonton Max, one of Canada's maximum security federal penitentiaries. After our first song no one clapped. Then the second song with still no applause. I was sweating, wondering what was going on. Then we played a Johnny Paycheck song called "Eleven Months and Twenty-Nine Days" and finally one big guy in the middle started clapping slowly, then the whole place followed. What a relief that was. That was probably one of the most awkward but rewarding shows we ever did.

When we arrived at Edmonton Max, I was still not quite awake and hungover from partying all night. The young Indigenous guy who had booked us to play there was part of the Indian Brotherhood at the jail; his name was Pelletier from Peguis First Nation in Manitoba. Before the concert I was having a casual conversation with him as I was getting coffee. He was telling me that there was some excitement in the population of the jail that week as someone had gotten out. I still did not catch the significance of that and so he reminded me that it was a maximum-security penitentiary and that the majority of the population was lifers so for someone to be getting released was a big deal. I then casually asked him when he was getting out and his answer was in thirty-two years. I was stunned and quite shaken at the thought of his extraordinary sentence. I felt weak in the knees but managed to catch the corner of the coffee stand to balance myself.

Thirty-two more years! I had trouble breathing, so I went to the back where the stage was and sat down on my amp to try to get myself together. The reality struck me hard as the guy was the same age as me, but I would be walking out of this hellhole in the next three hours not thirty-two years. The psychologist that was working guard duty for the show that afternoon came and asked me if I was going to be OK. I replied, "I guess we'll see."

Fast forward some three decades. I was looking for a place for our AA group to meet when I found a little white church on Manitoba and Powers right in the gritty war zone of the North End of Winnipeg. It was perfect, so I thought it would be a good idea for me to attend the mass there because the pastor, Pastor Paul, had been so gracious in having us move into his building to host our AA group. So, on a beautiful Sunday morning in June of 2017, I went to mass at the Living Word Temple. Pastor Paul asked me if I would sing "I Wanna Fly." During the mass, I noticed a gentleman seated a few rows down on my right. He was looking at me from time to time and flashed me a smile on one occasion. He looked familiar, but I just could not place him. He had a certain sparkle in his eye and so I concluded that something must have caused him to become so calm and peaceful. At the end of the service when I got up to leave, the gentleman approached me and asked, "Are you C-Weed?" and I replied, "Yes I am." He then said, "You played at Edmonton Max thirty-two years ago" and I replied "Yes" again. He then said, "I was the kid that called you to play for us, my last name is Pelletier." I gave him a big, long hug and wept openly. He had done his time and made it out. Turned out he had just been released the previous week. "I'm going to minister to a small congregation in a little town north of The Pas." He told me, "God is good." Good indeed.

I remember we packed the legendary Horseshoe Tavern on Yonge Street in Toronto. Bryan made the deal. We were playing in the area and we needed a place where we could house and feed ten people (our band and crew) from Monday to Thursday till our next show in

Manitoulin Island, so Bryan pitched the band to Randy, the owner. He was already booked for the weekend so Bryan told him we'd play Monday and Tuesday for rooms and meals. Randy told Bryan he never booked entertainment on those nights because they were his slowest nights of the week. He had no money to pay us for those nights. Bryan told him we'd play for free and just take the door, the cover charge. Randy could have the bar sales. He was skeptical at first but had nothing to lose. On the Monday the place was packed full, 465 people at a $10 cover charge. And we drew a huge lineup on Tuesday. We made over $10,000 for those Monday and Tuesday nights. The club owner was completely stunned by the numbers we drew. This kind of thing went on everywhere.

I played a CTV television show in Toronto entitled *Honky Tonk* that ran from 1981 to 1982. The host was none other than Rompin' Ronnie Hawkins and the set was kitted out to look like a honky-tonk saloon. I got flown to Toronto first class and waited in the front of the airport where I was told I would be picked up. I was watching for a car. A stretch limousine pulled up but I just went back inside to wait for the call. All of a sudden, the limo door opened and the driver asked, "Are you C-Weed?" "Oh, yeah," I said. He said, "I'm here to pick you up." I felt kind of silly riding in this big limo like I was on some star trip. I slouched down in the back in case someone saw me, an Indian, in there. I don't know why the hell I was worried, who would know me in Toronto?

Once we completed *The Finest You Can Buy* album, Slidin' Clyde Roulette officially joined the band on lead guitar. He was a great player in the bluesy southern rock style and really enlivened our shows with a rockier edge. He was a great guy to work with and Indigenous like the rest of us. With Clyde playing the rockier sound on guitar and Jim Flett pure country, our repertoire covered a lot of musical taste during that period of our musical development. Clyde was the opposite of Jimmy Flett in that he wanted to get out the road. He was ready to travel.

Clyde was with us when we recorded our second album, *High And Dry*. We continued to record (and pay the costs ourselves) at Century 21 working with the Hildebrand brothers, but we also did some recording at Roade Studios, a small recording facility located on the second and third floors of an old house in suburban Crescentwood in south Winnipeg, working with Glen Axford, another fine engineer.

The title song, "High And Dry," was a cover of a Rolling Stones track composed by Mick Jagger and Keith Richards from their 1966 album *Aftermath*. We gave it a bit more of a country sound and it became another hit single for us, reaching the Top 10 right across the country in 1982. We also covered songs from Chuck Berry ("Memphis"), the granddaddy of country music Hank Williams ("Cold, Cold Heart"), Fred Oleson ("A Little Bit of Lovin' Tonight") and one of my favourite singer/songwriters Rodney Crowell (his classic "Ain't Living Long Like This"). My confidence was growing more and more as a songwriter and, as a result, I contributed five of my own songs to the album, "Loving You," "One More Day With You," "New Mexico," "A Long Time Before Today" and also, "I Heard The Owl Call My Name," which was inspired by the Margaret Craven book of the same name.

Back out on the road, Clyde was having problems. He was married and was having a hard time with his wife back home about his being away so much. He was on the phone arguing with her every night. He finally left the band in Ottawa, returning home to Winnipeg. The band and crew were holed up at Bryan's house in Wendover, Ontario, just a half hour east of Ottawa, where he was still working for the Secretary of State. We had a lot of fun hanging out with Bryan and his family. Myralene made hash cake and DH (her brother Donald Henderson, our light man) jumped into Bryan's swimming pool except there was a thin sheet of ice, he popped up on the opposite end of the pool through the ice, fun times. We had gigs

lined up going east into the Maritimes, so on short notice we hired
Billy Joe Green to complete the tour. Billy Joe was great, a brilliant
player and a real showman. We completed that tour and returned
home. Billy Joe was a temporary fix. We needed permanent guitar
player and we lucked out by getting a guitar player and a fiddle player
in one. I remembered seeing the Dutiaume Brothers at the Centennial
Concert Hall and was impressed with young Clint. I contacted him
and he was keen to join us. Clint was only seventeen, so he got the
nickname The Kid. We picked him up along the highway in Richer,
Manitoba where he is from and off we went to Halifax. He turned
into a solid guitar player and also added fiddle to our live sound. I
remember we came back to Winnipeg after the tour and we were
booked to play the Stock Exchange Hotel. Clint was still underage,
so we ran the cables into the kitchen and he played his fiddle and
guitar from there. Clint finished his schooling then rejoined us and
stayed with the band for many years.

The early 1980s were a whirlwind for the group. We were a pretty
big deal on a national level. But everything just blew out of the water
in 1983 with our third album, *Going The Distance*. This time I contributed six songs. We again recorded the tracks at Century 21 but we
mixed it in Edmonton. At this point, Craig Fotheringham was deeply
involved with the band, producing and mixing the album (with
Wally), playing on the tracks and co-writing some of the songs with
me. Craig was a musical genius from Dryden, Ontario who moved
to Winnipeg in the mid-1970s and quickly became an in-demand
piano and guitar player both live and in the studio before becoming a top-flight record producer for local country artists. His slow,
soft-spoken manner belied a musical mind that was always ahead of
everyone else. Craig brought much to the C-Weed Band along with
a key connection. His older brother Jim, a former Winnipeg musician, was now an executive at RCA Records in Toronto. Through
Craig's intervention on our behalf with his brother, we signed with
RCA Canada. That was a giant step up for us. After signing with

RCA records, we began to get all the big opening-act opportunities like opening for Waylon Jennings at the old Winnipeg arena. I spent time with Waylon after that and saw him at different shows. We kept in touch with each other. We also opened for Hoyt Axton at the Centennial Concert Hall. We got the nod from Gilles Paquin to play at the inaugural Beaver Dam Lake Music Festival, opening for Hank Williams Jr. and Dickie Betz. Also included in a large show run, we were called to perform three years in a row at the We Fest in Detroit Lakes, Minnesota. There we shared the stage with George Jones, The Charlie Daniels Band (who spent most of the afternoon on our bus), John Anderson, and many other folks that we got to rub elbows with backstage. We were also invited to perform at the The Big Valley Jamboree in Craven, Saskatchewan, where I got to spend some quality time with Willie Nelson on his tour bus. We talked to about 4 A.M. then we all drove together to the Regina airport where I had to drop off my car rental and Willie and six crew members were catching his private jet. They were told at the airport that they had one too many people to legally fly at night, so I got my car rental back and told the extra guy to jump in the car rental and we chased down their tour bus at Albert and Ring Rd. I returned to the airport and let Willie know that I had gotten his crew member onto the bus and then they left on his jet and the boys picked me up with our bus and off we went into the night. All of us going in different directions to our respective next shows.

The reggae/calypso arrangement of "Magic In The Music" was Craig's idea. He had been working with singer George McCrea on an album at Century 21 recording studios, which he had booked for three months. George scored a huge international hit with the disco song "Rock Your Baby" and was now living in Winnipeg (and working in the meat department of a grocery chain in town) after marrying a Winnipeg girl. Craig was all into reggae/calypso when we came in to record "Magic in The Music." He took my nice little country rock song and arranged it into a reggae/calypso thing with synthesizers playing steel drum sounds. It was an autobiographical song about my life. When I heard it after he arranged it, all I could think of was "What the fuck did you do to my song?!" I was fuming in the hallway of the studio, ready to walk out. That caused some friction between Craig and me. I was seriously upset and didn't want it on the album. My brother-in-law, Jimmy Shuttleworth, who had nothing to do with music whatsoever, came to the studio one night when we just happened to be mixing the album. He heard "Magic in The Music" and afterwards he took me aside and said, "That's gonna be your biggest hit." I said, "Oh, great, I guess." I hated playing it for a long time. Ironically that's the song that earned us a Juno nomination. That certainly changed my opinion of it.

Magic in the Music

Too many miles too long on the road
16 Hours with five more to go
A dozen one-night stands in the two weeks we been gone
No you don't understand I been at this way to long
Just one last tour tasting the lure of the road
But wait listen I can feel it coming on
The reason we all do it now it's coming on real strong
Whoa wait that's it

Listen for the Magic in the Music
The crowd hustles in the show's about to begin
They're playing our song guess it's time to go on
Those first few minutes always scare me half to death
My body's a shaken and my hands are filled with sweat
Just one last tour tasting the lure of the road
But wait listen I can feel it coming on

The reason we all do it now it's coming on real strong
Whoa wait that's it listen for the magic in the Music
Listen for the Magic in the music
Take it to your soul you'll never lose it
Treat it like your best friend don't abuse it
And we live for the magic in the Music

Going The Distance yielded four Top Ten hit singles: "Play Me My Favorite Song," "Bringing Home The Good Times," "Pickup Truck Cowboy," and "Magic in The Music," all composed by me. At the annual MCMA (Manitoba Country Music Association) awards in 1983 the C-Weed Band walked off with seven awards. We took home everything except Female Vocalist. That was such a rush to receive that kind of recognition in our home province. More significantly, we were competing for these awards equally with non-Indigenous artists and judged solely on our music, not our race. There was no segregation. We were also nominated for Junos awards: Country Band of The Year and Country Album of the Year. The following year we were nominated for Country Music Song of The Year for "Magic In The Music," and best group or duo. We didn't win, but nonetheless those were heady days, indeed.

The sound on *Going The Distance* was light years ahead of our previous albums. I credit Wally for that, he and Craig. Wally was persistent in getting the sound right, whereas Craig would have said it was good enough. We actually took the two-inch master tapes with us to Edmonton since we had a gig there at the Cook County Saloon. Wally wanted to mix them at Damon Studios. I was angry because I wanted to get the album out as soon as possible and didn't want to delay it in any way. But Wally knew what he was doing, and he was right. Damon Studios had a UK-built Neve control board, same as the board we recorded on at Century 21 studio, except this Neve had the computerized mix down. Sliders that you set and they move on their own by computer. Man, we loved watching that. The studio was great for rock music and that was our sound. Wally spent a lot of time on that album, hours and hours getting the sound right on *Going The Distance*. He wouldn't leave it until he had every song sounding perfect. Everybody we knew in the music business was awestruck by the sound we had on that album.

The cover photo, taken by Clint, was of our renovated 1953 Western Flyer bus that we had outfitted for band travel. That bus was our home. The camaraderie we had between the band and our crew was special. It was like all for one and one for all and our crew was just as much a part of the family as my brothers, Clyde and Clint. We thought we would go on forever. When we arrived in a town or a reserve, people could see that camaraderie when they saw us. Fred Hays, Indigenous and my first cousin, was our sound man. Donald Henderson, our light guy, was a relative as well. My brother Bryan and my sister Delphine both married into the Henderson family and Donald was another sibling. We also travelled with our own cook, Roger Lamoureux. We had a stove on the bus and we would stop at a campsite and Roger would serve up a stew or something. Having Roger along saved us a lot of money on the road. Sometimes we were refused service in restaurants, so this was a way to avoid that.

I took the bookings, dealt with the buyers and paid everybody in the band. All that is what a manager does. This was long before cellphones so I would be in a phone booth in the pouring rain returning calls while the other guys were high and dry relaxing on the bus. The band was never an equal partnership because I did all the business. That created some resentment. But the success of our business model, which I learned from Stirling years ago, led to other Indigenous bands adopting my template to run their business. But some of them started taking deposits for shows in advance, then not showing up for the show. That kind behavior hurt all of us Indigenous bands, the C-Weed Band included. Buyers became wary of giving deposits for fear of having a no-show. We were never a no-show, but it took some time for me to sort that all out with a few skeptical buyers.

A huge thrill for me came when we played in Regina for a Center of The Arts concert. Buffy Sainte-Marie was playing at the Regina Folk Festival at the same time. She had finished up her set and unbeknownst to us, came by the Arts Center. We were onstage doing our last set. I was up front singing "Can't You See." Suddenly I heard this angelic voice coming out of my monitor. I looked around and there was Buffy on our stage. She came on just to sing that song with us. In 1998 The C-Weed Band played with Buffy at the T'Saille College Campus in Arizona for the American Indian Music Festival. I found it odd that Buffy, who was top billing, went on at five in the afternoon, while we were slotted in after midnight. But it turned out that the crowd was at its peak in the early evening. Later, when the sun was down, it was extremely cold and there weren't many people left in the audience. I didn't realize that the desert got really cold overnight. Don's son Mike Bruyere later joined Buffy's band along with other local Indigenous musicians, Jesse Green on guitar and Leroy Constant on bass guitar.

We were excited to receive a booking at the Hall of Fame Inn in Nashville, Tennessee. We played shows on the way down, including in Wisconsin and Denver. But our appearance in Nashville caused quite a big stir. It was just like they said in the movies, a guy came up to me and he's got a suitcase with what looked to me like about $10,000 cash in it. All this money piled up, packets of bills. He wanted to negotiate with me for my songs. Record labels and song publishers in Nashville are so hungry for songs that they're always on the lookout for songwriters and willing to pay big money for original songs. People think Nashville is all about singers, but it's all about songs. Singers are a dime a dozen, but you need to have songs for them to sing and record. As soon as these music business types heard us playing, they loved the band, but they were more interested in the songs we played. When they learned that I was the guy who wrote them, they came to see me right away. "What are you going to do with these songs?" they asked me. I told them, "No, they're not for sale."

I wasn't going to play that game. There was talk of us opening for Alabama on a big national tour, but nothing came of it. We played a few more gigs then came home.

∞

In the latter part of the 1970s we had started playing fairly regularly at the Downs Hotel way out Portage Avenue west just before the perimeter highway in Winnipeg. The bar was known as Ma's Corral for the woman who ran the place, Elizabeth 'Ma' Henning. Ma was larger than life and a force to be reckoned with. A big German woman, she wielded considerable influence in the local country music scene and by force of will and ego turned the Downs into the hot spot for country music in Winnipeg. She saw how popular we were when we played her club. We packed the place every night. Ma badly wanted to get her clutches on us. She envisioned herself as our manager and Svengali. Ma was a huge self-promoter; it was all about her, always. Somehow Craig Fotheringham was tied into Ma through her Downs Records label. With Craig on her side and now as a member of the band, we recorded the 1985 album *Live at Ma's* for RCA Records that featured songs from our first three albums done live. We took some flak for having Craig in the band because he was white. He was also starting to exert too much influence over our sound.

Ma made us an offer to become our manager. As far as I was concerned, we had been doing just fine with me serving as manager and didn't need anyone from outside muscling in. We had a rebellious attitude and didn't put up with the racism in the music scene. We were a band of Indians who didn't do what others told us to do. Plus being brothers, we were tighter, more close-knit, than other bands. We didn't think we needed Ma. But she sweetened the proposition with a significant loan for us to buy more gear and transportation and a guarantee of a long-term booking at her Corral. Despite my skepticism, we took the bait and signed contracts with her. It would turn out to be a deal with the devil. We were now deeply in debt to her and had no say in decisions affecting the band and our well-being.

Racking up MACA awards and Juno nominations along with a half dozen hit singles, our stock was rising and others in the music business took notice. A local consortium of power players in the business approached me with an offer to take over management. These guys—booking agents Gilles Paquin, Bruce 'Bones' Rathbone and ex-Winnipeg Mayor Sam Katz—had the connections to take us to the next level in our career. They could do more than Ma or I could do for us. They were the heavyweights in the entertainment business in Winnipeg as well as nationally and internationally. They didn't want to change us or harness our energy; they wanted to take all that made us a good band and move it forward. They approached me and laid out their proposals for management. I looked at all of it and realized the potential of having these guys behind the band. But I also knew that we had a problem. We had signed deals with Ma Henning. She had her hooks deep into us. She didn't want anyone else booking the C-Weed Band. She did it by throwing money at us that we readily spent on a truck and a bus plus the biggest Martin PA sound system around. With all this we had moved into a whole other level of production compared to our contemporaries. But there was a price to be paid, and it was an exclusive agreement to play Ma's venue. She had a lock on us. I urged the others to go with Paquin, Rathbone and Katz, but Wally wanted to stay with Ma Henning. Ma proved to be the kiss of death for us. In the ensuing disagreement, the band split in two, with me on one side and Wally, Don and Clint on the other. I refused to be pushed around by Ma Henning. Wally disagreed. There was bitterness and recrimination between us. The proposal from the heavyweights disappeared.

Those contracts with Ma followed me around for years and the only way I could get out from under them in the end was to file for bankruptcy protection. Her son was a lawyer and he never wanted to let go of their hold on me.

I carried on as C-Weed and signed with fledgling local record label Thunder Records, which was a partnership between entertainment lawyer David Wolinsky and ex-Bachman-Turner Overdrive member Fred Turner. Unfortunately Thunder Records didn't last long, but I did manage to record one of my best songs for them. With the release of "I Wanna Fly," my songwriting skills moved up to "world class," according to Fred Turner.

Later, Wally, Don and Clint tried to use the C-Weed Band name. They would take bookings as "formerly of C-Weed," but bookers would simply bill them as C-Weed. Without me there was no C-Weed, just a band of guys who used to be in the C-Weed Band. I brought an injunction against them to stop using the name. It wasn't really their fault; it was unscrupulous club owners trying to capitalize on our good name. They then became Freebird. Although Don came back to play with me a few years later and has stayed to this day, and Clint came back after spending time with his brothers in The Younger Brothers band (they scored a few hit singles including "A Good Day To Ride"), I didn't play with Wally again for over twenty years. Being brothers, we saw each other from time to time when family members got together, but we didn't talk much during those years. He made his decision and I mine. I kept the name alive, working all the time. It was on my shoulders. He chose to walk away.

In those intervening years I think we both did some growing up, Wally and me. We both look back and agree that we blew it. Wally is still my brother and even though we've had our differences, I've depended on him a lot. Our differences were about business, nothing personal, just business.

It had been a wild ride those past seven years or so, like a rollercoaster with plenty of ups and downs. But one thing remained consistent and that was our absolute dedication to the music. We may have compromised a potential future but we never compromised our music. We broke down the doors that had for decades barred Indigenous singers and musicians from the Canadian music mainstream. In doing so we became role models and inspirations to Indigenous people young and old across Canada and into the USA.

We never played the 'Indian card'. We never rode on Indigenous coattails. We let our music speak for itself. If you heard our records but didn't know anything about the band you would never have thought we were an Indigenous band. That was important to us. It was always about the music. Our songs didn't deal with the Indigenous experience. We were not trying to draw attention to Indigenous issues until "Run As One" released in 2000. Our music spoke for us, and it was good music so we rose above any racism.

One particular memory will remain with me forever. After performing at the Calgary Stampede in the early 1980s, we pulled into Richmond, BC just outside Vancouver in our bus to play at the BC Country Music Awards. We'd driven all night over the mountains. I checked into our hotel and brought my suitcase and guitar to my room before heading back downstairs to get something to eat. I went to the café in the hotel and as I sat down to order, an Aboriginal family walked in the front door, parents and two kids, a boy and a girl. As they walked by my table, one of the kids tugged on his dad's coat and said, "There's that guy who was on TV." It stunned me. Here I was on the west coast, Vancouver for all intents and purposes, and someone recognized me. It might have been my trademark black hat, I don't know. But I was spotted in this little hotel café. At that moment I remembered back to the map I had looked at in elementary school and thinking I would never, ever be able to make it all the way to Vancouver. Now here I was, I had made it that far, and someone had recognized me from a Country Music show taped in Regina, Saskatchewan and aired on CBC television, the Neeche kid from Eddystone.

CHAPTER 4

I Wanna Fly

Alcoholism is part of our genetics and part of our lifestyle as Indigenous people. Alcohol and drug addiction problems ran in our family. All the siblings suffered addictions at one time or another. But there wasn't a lot of liquor in our house because there was no liquor store in Eddystone. You had to go to Ste. Rose du Lac, which wasn't always easy. Also, alcohol was expensive and my parents didn't have a lot of money. They drank. Just not every day. Errol and our brother Randy used to drink to excess at a very early age. For them it wasn't about having a drink to have some fun, they drank to get wasted as fast as they could. Later, Errol brought cocaine into the band.—*Wally Ranville*

I didn't know at the time how bad Errol's cocaine addiction was. I never paid much attention to any symptoms of addiction he might have been showing. Cocaine addicts can hide it well. But drugs were all around us. We used to take a lot of bennies on the road just to keep up the pace. We thought they were keeping us going but they were slowing us down. We eventually quit all the drugs because of the effect it was having on us, personally and as a band. —*Don Ranville*

When Errol saw that I was having a problem with the drinking, he did not criticize me. He did not ostracize me. He never scolded me nor shook his finger at me. He was always in support of my recovery. That is all I can say about him, that he supported my recovery when I first started to recover. Recovery is huge in the music industry because we depend on the alcohol or drugs for so long. It's like saying goodbye to a friend. Sometimes you need support to do that. Errol gave me lots of support during my time of early recovery and I am always grateful to him for that. —*Billy Joe Green, musician*

For Indigenous people, alcohol is a curse. It always has been and continues to be. The image of the drunken Indian plagues us, haunts us, and follows us to this day and beyond. We are stigmatized by that image. That's how many white people regard us and until we can overcome that, we will continue to be marginalized in North American society. I saw it first-hand in my community growing up. And it was in my home, too. It's easy for Indigenous people to succumb to alcohol abuse, to give up their self-esteem and self-worth to a bottle and become the stereotype. We have to break the cycle of alcohol addiction just as we have to break the cycle of poverty and apathy. Music artists are more visible in society as well as in our Indigenous communities, so it is that much more important that we lead the charge in combating alcoholism and addictions.

Looking back at it now, there was no defence mechanisms of any kind in and around Eddystone. The booze came into the community, and in a lot of ways alcohol was used to control the community. I saw alcohol and I saw alcoholics very early on around my family. Some people took advantage of the desire that people had for alcohol and their addiction. My dad worked hard. People hired him to do carpentry work because he was good, a craftsman. But he never got paid what he should have got paid for his work. In the community, some people knew that cases of beer went a lot further.

Dad was a drinker. Alcoholism was present in our family. But my mother never drank until the last child, Donna, was born. Mom was forty-two when my sister Donna was born. She started drinking more or less just to be with Dad. The beverage room at the Ste. Rose Hotel, the Rainbow Room, was the place Dad would go to drink publicly. He would be there all night on Saturday nights. So eventually Mom started drinking to be with him. Those were dark days. It was hard to see your parents and other adults in that condition. We would catch a ride with them to Ste. Rose where we would hang out and hustle other kids while they drank in the Rainbow Room.

There was always the fear that someone might get hurt. There was no negotiating when they were drunk, so we knew to get out of the house when things got tense. Alcohol brought violence into our home. It became a negative factor in our house and things could get ugly. Fortunately, my parents stopped drinking once we moved to Winnipeg.

My mother's brother, Angus Spence, was the first in our extended family to get sober. He had a successful cattle business and had a lot to lose, so he cleaned himself up. I remember seeing the AA book (Alcoholics Anonymous' Twelve- Step Program) at his place. We used to walk to his house every Saturday evening to watch *Hockey Night In Canada* and again on Sundays to watch *The Ed Sullivan Show*. He had the only TV in the family for a time. You didn't sit in Angus's chair. You could sit anywhere but his chair was sacrosanct. Uncle Angus's Alcoholics Anonymous book was always out on the arm of his chair. We kind of walked around that book, giving it a wide berth. We knew what it was, but its presence right there in front of us for all to see was unnerving. Growing up in a community where alcoholism was rampant, I saw alcoholism all around me and I also saw recovery and that was my uncle Angus. I loved that guy for creating a path to freedom for us all.

The other extended family members, Angus's family, were wary of him after he got sober because he would tell them in no uncertain terms to clean up their lives. They would hide the booze when he was coming over. I loved Angus. He was a great role model for me, the kind of guy who if he saw a problem, he got it fixed. He helped start the Manitoba Métis Federation. He called the chiefs and started that whole institution. He was destined to be someone bigger than Eddystone. The others in the family resented him because he had money and they didn't. And they wanted it. I remember hearing him tell his siblings that money is just a bunch of paper. It's not worth anything. If you spend it, it's gone and then you really have nothing. He went on, "If there was a million dollars on the table right here, you'd all take it and spend it. Then what have you got? Just a bunch of stuff and the money's all gone. But if you take that million dollars and invest it, only then does it have value because only then does it go to work for you. Your money is making money for you." I was still young but that message resonated with me even though I had to look up what investing meant.

I started drinking at a very early age. I was about ten when I started, but by age twelve, I was a falling down drunk. When I drank, I drank like an alcoholic and I would go crazy. I made friends at St. Rose school and on some weekends, I would stay with them. We had fun but a lot of that fun involved alcohol, just teenager stuff getting drunk and feeling sick the next morning. When I started performing in the community with my brothers, I used to get terrible stage fright before I went on. I was in my teens. Dad would get a bottle of lemon gin and I would knock half the bottle down, then go out and do the show. It became a crutch and I knew it, but I thought I needed it. That started the cycle. Alcohol was part and parcel of my being a musician.

Booze was the killer in the Brunswick Hotel days. I can remember getting a warm beer at nine cents a glass across the street at the Leland Hotel before I would make my appearance at the Brunswick. I would get the shakes around 1:00 P.M., 1:30, the show started at 3:00. We played from 3:00 to 6:00, then back for 9:00 to 12:00 A.M. (later 1:00 A.M.). We were surrounded by alcohol at the Brunswick. Everyone wants to buy the singer a beer. Come by their table and they want to buy you a beer just to have you sit with them. It was like a party every night. That was my first experience with the bad hangover and not being able to get up the next day. On occasion I was too drunk to play and I knew it wasn't good. I remember someone telling me that I was too drunk to go onstage. I was still in my teens. That might have been my moment of epiphany, being told I was too drunk to play. That's when I sought out help. I saw the dark side of alcohol and got out of it early because I wanted to be a musician more than I wanted to be a drunk. I got out of that lifestyle but so many other guys I knew back then didn't. I'm still standing while many of them aren't.

I first went to AA at age sixteen but I didn't stay. I went back at age twenty and sobered up and stayed sober from addictions for 12½ years. February 14, 1974 was the day I became sober. My desire to sing and be in a band was stronger than my desire to drink. I was lucky, I had a goal. You can't sing in a band if you're falling off a stage, so I reached out to AA. There was alcohol everywhere around me, especially playing bars and reserves, but I knew I didn't want to destroy my life like others around me. The guys in the band eventually got sober as well. We still smoked dope, but we weren't drinking. Hey, it's legal now. We were ahead of the curve, so we thought.

During my drinking years I became a father. I was sixteen years of age. The girl, Georgina Maytwayashing, was twenty-one and Dakota Sioux from Winnipeg. Her family was from the Dog Creek Reserve on Lake Manitoba. We met just before we moved to Winnipeg. The Seaweed and the Weeds Band came to the city to play a show at the Indian and Métis Friendship Center. We began a relationship and our son Derek was born in 1970 in Winnipeg. I needed to grow up fast but I made a mess of it. We never married, she raised Derek on her own with support from her family. I was hammered all the time and it was best that he not be around me. I understood. It was a safety thing, a precaution. Her parents didn't want him around me, which was the right thing to do. I reconnected with Derek when he was age nine, after I got sober. He would come over to my house on Burrows Avenue and we got to know one another. Georgina and I remained friends and her family never turned Derek away from me. They loved me and still do. I am part of that family. Derek is married now with two children, my grandchildren, Brandan and Amber, and drives a long-haul rig between Winnipeg and Brandon. He is a vital part of my life in more ways than one as he is my sound tech and I won't play a show without him there. Wally taught him how to set up the sound system and mix the sound and now he is indispensable to the band. Derek still earns a considerable side income for mixing sound for different organizations so Wally once again, like in the case of teaching our first cousin Fred Hayes, has fulfilled the age-old parable, "if you feed a man a fish you feed him for a day, if you teach him how to fish you feed him for a lifetime," I am forever grateful to my brother Wally.

I proudly remained alcohol free until another addictive substance came into my life and took hold of me. As I described in the previous chapter, in 1986 I was booked to appear on CTV's *Honky Tonk* television show filmed in Toronto. On the show, I duetted with host Ronnie Hawkins and his band. At the after party in a nearby Chinese restaurant, I was leaving the biffy when Ronnie pushed me back into the washroom and into a stall. I had no idea what he was up to. It felt odd being in a washroom stall with another man, but he sat backward on the toilet and started pouring out this white powder on the top of the toilet tank. He started chopping it up into lines with a razor; I had no idea what he was up to. Keep in mind, I had never seen cocaine before. I'd heard of it, but never saw it. I certainly knew about dope and speed and a lot of highs like acid in the 60s. Ronnie then rolled up a twenty-dollar bill and handed it to me. I had no clue what to do. I didn't want to look naïve and embarrass myself, so I said to him, "You go first, it's your stuff." I watched what he was doing as he snorted up a couple of lines before handing me the bill. So, I did what he did. Man, what an incredible buzz. All you need to do is try it once and you're hooked. I tell people, "Don't even try it because you'll be hooked instantly."

I came back to Winnipeg the next day, and all I had in my head was how I could get more of that shit. It was all I could think about. Cocaine wasn't around as much then as it is now, but it wasn't that hard to score. The dealers in the city who were selling me dope for years were more than happy to supply me with cocaine. More money for them because, unlike dope, you get hooked on it right away. You're always chasing that initial buzz. Once I started doing it, people around me started doing it, too, including the guys in the band. They didn't want to be left out. I opened the doors to cocaine addiction for a lot of people, which I am not very proud of.

Cocaine takes over your life. From the time you wake up in the morning, your focus is on scoring cocaine. It became a serious problem for me. I was still okay to do shows, at least I thought I was, but it took a toll on my health. You don't eat when you're addicted to coke. I used to drink a forty-ounce bottle of Jack Daniels just to come down enough from the coke to get some sleep. No one could find me at times and that is how I wanted it. My lifetime friend, Andre "Jigs' Henderson used to bring me two forty-ounce Jack Daniels to get to sleep while I was holed up at what is now the Quest Inn on Ellice and Hargrave in Winnipeg. I was hiding out there with $2,800 in cash and an ounce of cocaine. Jigs was the only one who knew where I was hiding that whole week. I don't think he really wanted to bring me the booze or even keep from telling anyone where I was hiding. He just loved me unconditionally and did whatever I asked him to do. Andre has been jokingly referred to as my sidekick for over fifty years. He has travelled with us in the band since the release of the "Going the Distance" album in 1983. Andre saved my life more than a few times while I was bingeing. So, I was back on the bottle as well as the coke. My life was total madness by this point. And yet I was still trying to keep up the façade that everything was cool and I was in control of myself. Then I missed a show, and I never missed shows. I was the iron man of the band so to speak. No matter how sick I was, flu, coughing, whatever, I always showed up to play. The band was playing The Downs Motor Inn, full house, and I was at home, coked out. I couldn't move. Fortunately, Sonny Bandura was in the audience that night and he got up and did the show with the band. Then I missed a second show.

I thought I was never going to get off that shit. It was going to kill me. I would stop for three days and congratulate myself. Then I'd start all over again. Then it was six days sober, feeling good, then back again. I was like a yoyo. It went on like this, but the sober stretches started getting longer and longer. I had a good support system around me cheering me on during the sober stretches, two weeks then three months. Then I was sober for seven months but fell down again.

My epiphany came from my brother Bryan, my saviour. He has always been in my corner. I was living in my little house on Burrows Avenue. The blinds were all pulled down and the place was a disaster. I was down on my knees on the floor snorting up white lint, my nose was bleeding from being cracked and dry from dirt and dog hair on the floor. That's how bad it was. That's how Bryan found me. Bryan didn't do drugs. He walked in and I was on the floor, a total wreck. He was standing there looking down at me and he said, "There are going to be a lot of little brown faces all across the country really disappointed. Another successful Indian bites the dust." Then he walked out. Oh man, I felt so bad. His words pierced my heart. It was tough love and I needed to hear it. That was a turning point for me. The next day I went back to AA and got the help I needed to get sober again. March 22, 1989 is my sober date and I've been clean of cocaine and alcohol ever since, over thirty-one years now. It was only 2 ½ years of cocaine addiction, but it did its damage. The other guys in the band cleaned up soon after.

I don't think I would have gotten sober had it not been for music. The spirit of the music was much stronger than my addictions. Music saved me. It always did. It saved me from myself. The fans and the

Indigenous leaders, they pulled me out of going the wrong way. They got me facing the right way. I remember I had been sober for seven months and Leslie and I were driving home from Maddock Recording Studio and listening to the unmixed version of "I Wanna Fly," on the CD player in the van, and I remember thinking "I believe I'm off that shit for good." That was October 1989.

Long-term relationships are difficult to maintain for musicians. You're away for long stretches of time and when you're around, the focus is always on you, not her. It's hard for a woman to accept that kind of life, alone much of the time and in the shadows the rest. The reality for me is that I'm married to the stage. There's no place for a woman because my love and passion go to the stage. I leave it all on that stage. It is hard for a partner to compete with that. Southern rocker Toy Caldwell of the Marshall Tucker Band once said, "the stage is the God-darndest woman I have ever known." I concur.

I had had lots of flings with women by the time I met Leslie Moszynski at the annual St. James Buffalo Barbecue. She was a brunette and taller than me. It was 1978. She wasn't Indigenous. We were playing an afternoon set. I was up onstage and when I looked out into the audience our eyes met. There was an immediate connection between us, a chemistry. That same night she showed up at our gig at Ma's Corral. Afterwards we talked and I gave her my phone number. Sure enough, a day or two later she called me and we embarked on a relationship that lasted nineteen years. They say that opposites attract so that must have been the case with Leslie and me. We were opposites. She was more cautious about her spending, where I spent just about every cent I got. She had a job and got up in the morning, while I came home in the morning and went to bed. We shared a love of music and went to lots of concerts together. Leslie was around in my cocaine addiction years but she never used it. She once flushed my $450 rock of cocaine down the toilet. I was fit to be tied.

We never married—I would have but she never wanted to—but we lived together at my house on Burrows Avenue. She was content to stay in a common-law relationship so I was okay with that. The house was modest, but I was comfortable in it. Friends would say to me, "You're a big star and you live in this little house?" That kind of thing never mattered to me. I have never been comfortable in an ostentatious lifestyle with lots of shiny things. I had a roof over my head and didn't care about having a big fancy house. I think that came from my upbringing. I didn't feel I had to compete with anyone. Before that I had been living in a house on Polson Avenue with Wally, Don, and two girls, a real party house. I spent my money on guitars.

Leslie had a good government job, but she left it to travel with me. When I opened up a series of C-Weeds cabarets, she helped out with the administration, office management, and handled the accounting. I still did all the bookings and on-site operations at the cabarets. We worked well together, I thought. She helped me. I remained the creative force as well as the driving force, the one that kept the whole machine rolling. But she did the technical end and helped me with the actual making of contracts, little stuff that I did not do very well. We were a good partnership, but she was still in my shadow.

Was it the rock 'n roll lifestyle that drove us apart? I think it was. Under those circumstances, any relationship is bound to get strained. I was gone for three months at a time. I think the reason why our relationship thrived was because we weren't always together. There were no problems because I was on the road probably at least half of those nineteen years. Maybe that's why it worked for that long. You can't have problems if you're not together. For most of the relationship, I would be coming home. That was always nice. I come home and we would grab onto each other and hold on. So, of course, it did not take long for eighteen or nineteen years to get behind us in a situation like that. But after a while I could see that it was not that rewarding for her. The accolades were coming my way, the attention was coming my way, and she's getting lost in the whole thing. She was not getting a fair reward for her life and her commitment at that point. We grew apart. I just think that at that point it was over. We could not do for each other what we had done for each other in the years that had passed.

We got to a point where it just didn't work anymore. She wanted other things. And I would have rolled along in my old-fashioned way probably until I died. She was not prepared to stick it out. I'm no saint. I had my problems and I still do. I think I inherited my dad's anger and disposition. I always had an anger management issue. I admit I'm not the easiest guy to live with at times.

The hardest part of our split up, however, was her taking up with our fiddle/guitar player Clint Dutiaume. That was a painful blow. She connected with Clint at one of our shows. At that point the spark had gone out of our relationship. Obviously, the camaraderie Clint and I had enjoyed for years ended abruptly. Eventually Clint and I put the bad feelings behind us for the sake of the C-Weed Band and our families would always remain close. I believe we recognized that the band was bigger than any one member so that led us to an eventual reunion. My brothers Wally and Don played a big part in mediating and facilitating the band reunion. More about this later.

Anyway, at the time I moved in with my brother Wally taking the basement room formerly occupied by Clint. So, I was living in Clint's room and he was living in my room. I guess that is not funny, but it is kind of funny now and hey, that's the way it came down. After being in a relationship for nineteen years of course I was depressed for a time but determined to start over. I just needed to get out of Winnipeg for a while.

On the lookout for business opportunities and a chance to give a helping hand up for Indigenous musicians, in 1992 I opened the first C-Weeds cabaret in Winnipeg at 1111 Logan Avenue at McPhillips Street. I financed the club with my own money along with $70,000 support from Aboriginal Business Development and a loan of $30,000 from my mother which I paid back in full. Mom had received an insurance claim settlement and she was happy to lend me that money for the cabaret. For the three years that the club was running, I paid her back regularly, like clockwork. She wanted to help out and was pleased to loan me the money. I kept a folder titled "Mom's Money" where I kept track of all my payments to her. The landlord who owned the building where the cabaret was located gave me a back-loaded lease which gave me a chance to get up and running or I wouldn't have made it that first year.

I didn't play the cabaret a lot because I wanted to give younger Indigenous musicians a venue and a chance to be heard. That was one of my goals in opening C-Weed's Cabarets. Our clientele was almost exclusive Indigenous. I had signs posted in the cabaret saying, "thank you for supporting an Indigenous Business Venture."

When I opened the cabaret in Winnipeg, Wally started the band Freebird, recruiting Don, Clint, and singer Fred Mitchell and taking a long-running gig down the street at the Stock Exchange Hotel where the C-Weed band had often played in the past. My club sat empty for almost a year while my fans went to see Wally and Don's band. So eventually I booked Freebird and all those people who used to go see them at the Stock followed them to C-Weeds. After this slow start, I began getting the Indigenous baseball teams coming in after their games. I courted them by sponsoring several teams. They started bringing their friends in. People draw people, so when people would look inside, they'd see a crowd and want to come in. Slowly but surely the place would be packed and we were doing well. For a little club licensed for 248 patrons, I made tons of money. One year alone I took in $2.8 million. The only other club that made more money in the province for that year was The Thompson Inn, sometimes affectionately referred to as "The T.I.", or Treasure Island.

The success of the Winnipeg cabaret led me to look further afield. I opened C-Weeds cabarets in Thunder Bay and later in Edmonton. Being an absentee owner, you go into it knowing you're going to be ripped off by staff. Cash has no mother or father. It belongs to whoever has it in their hands. I hired Indigenous staff, but these kinds of things still went on. It's part of the nature of that business. I couldn't be in each of the clubs every day. The Thunder Bay club didn't last long. I got tangled up with Vietnamese brothers, one owned the building, one owned the business, and one owned the liquor license. After I signed the lease and bought the business, I legally had three months to apply for a liquor license of my own. I began operating on the liquor license that came with the business not knowing that the brother whose name was on the license had been charged with prostitution of underaged girls and had returned to Vietnam. After three months of running the business, the club was making a lot of money, so the owner of the building called the police and reported me operating the business without a license. After spending $100,000 on leasehold improvements and paying $55,000 for the business, I got raided by Thunder Bay's finest and charged for operating without a license. I retained a Métis lawyer from Fort William First Nation who received death threats and had her house shot at after she had filed the papers for a lawsuit against the two brothers. Rather than cause any more trouble for the lawyer in an ugly situation and having made a lot of money already, I walked away from it and I still had the Winnipeg cabaret.

When my relationship with Leslie came to an end, I needed a fresh start. I heard about a building that was available in Edmonton, so I flew out there with my son Derek. It was right at the end of the whole "boot-scootin' boogie" era. It was a large facility with no customers. The location was right across from the Northlands Coliseum on 118th Avenue. The C-Weed band was well known throughout Alberta. We worked across the province over the years and played some big shows there. Being situated right across the road from the Coliseum where the Edmonton Oilers skated, I was able to sell my sixty parking stalls around the nightclub for every home game, which paid for my season tickets for the Oilers games. So as far as my love of hockey is concerned, the nightclub was a big success. We also enjoyed success with promoting local Indigenous talent and bands, as well as bringing in bands from Winnipeg for the local audience to enjoy, such as Wally's Freebird band and Eagle and Hawk. We ran talent shows to promote emerging Indigenous singers and songwriters, so our musical footprint was felt by the local Indigenous community. The club began to get a reputation for having a drug-dealing operation, so I met with the Edmonton Police narcotic squad and on a Thursday night, we walked through the room with thirty cops and barred several known drug dealers from the premises. On Saturday night they burned down the building.

While waiting for the insurance settlement, I opened a club in Fort McMurray, oil country still booming at the time. I signed a bad lease with the owners, so it didn't last long, and I lost money on it. Then I opened C-Weeds Cabaret in Saskatoon after making a deal with the owners to lease the old A-frame rock club, and after extensive renovations we got the doors opened. That club was an instant success. The night we opened I played, and it was packed and stayed that way. The C-Weed Band sold more product and played more of the big shows in Saskatchewan than anywhere else back in the day. Saskatchewan has always loved the band. I had a real honest woman named Sharon manage the club in Saskatoon, so of course I received every penny that the business earned. An awesome lady. We also had a great staff and bad-ass security.

The drug scene was really growing in Saskatoon and there were rumours among young people that any kind of drug you were looking for was available at C-Weeds. That bothered me, so I closed it down. I lost my desire. Knowing that young people associated C-Weeds, my name and my club, with drugs spoiled it for me. Saskatoon was the last club to close. That was in the summer of 2001. I came home to Winnipeg when my grandson was born. That changed my world.

I opened these clubs with the goal of providing opportunities for other Indigenous artists to perform. As a result, I booked Indigenous acts, many of whom were just starting out, and held talent contests. In addition, I played the clubs from time to time. I was giving back to the Indigenous communities that had supported me and elevated me to the position I was in. I was using the C-Weed brand to help other Indigenous artists but I would need a different means of promoting young Indigenous talent. I would eventually get into a recording studio business.

When I moved to Edmonton, accompanying me was Jayne Martin who had worked at the Winnipeg club. Jayne was a nice girl, short with blond hair. She was from Winnipeg and, like Leslie, wasn't Indigenous. My relationship with Leslie ended in August; by October I was with Jayne. It was a rebound relationship. I was in a deep depression when Leslie left me, and Jayne was there. We married at a small ceremony in our backyard in Edmonton with a justice of the peace. The marriage was more or less a reaction to a big fight we had. I went out and bought a ring at the mall. Once we married, Jayne no longer worked. We were together for seven years. Like Leslie, it was another case of opposites. Jayne had her own hobbies and loved horses. We lived in Edmonton for three years then moved to Saskatoon to run the club there. We stayed in Saskatoon for three years before moving back to Winnipeg in 2001.

I was putting a new C-Weed band together in anticipation of heading out on the road again. While this was going on, Jayne became involved in a business deal with a local family who had a ranch near our place. I wasn't interested in investing in selling saddles and the like so that kind of created a wedge between Jayne and me. She wanted to pursue this possible business relationship so one day she just told me she wanted a divorce. That was in 2004. There again it was my anger disposition that brought an end to that bliss. Jayne got the house and the acreage in the divorce settlement. I moved into Winnipeg again and took up residence in Old St. Boniface. I admit I'm not the easiest person to be with at times. I do believe that the breakup was part of the pressure of being C-Weed, being like a fish in a bowl, a monkey in a zoo, for all those years. I had to live a certain way. People have seen me as a dollar sign my whole life. I was never really seen as a human being. I never really had any kind of true friendships. People see me as a star, they see me as money. Of course, I later realized that not all people saw me that way.

After Jayne and I divorced, I was a mess. I was in rough shape and depressed. Once again, my savior, my brother Bryan, came to my aid. The NDP was in power in Manitoba, and Eric Robinson was the Minister of Culture and Heritage. He was Indigenous from Cross Lake but had come to Winnipeg to work at the CBC. I knew Eric from when we were teenagers. I met him when I was playing at the Brunswick and we used to drink together. Eric was speaking at a luncheon, so Bryan suggested I go with him to see Eric. Bryan was now working for the provincial government. After the speech, Bryan urged me to go say hello to Eric. I hemmed and hawed, thinking Eric might not remember me but, in the end, I went over and tapped him on the shoulder. He turned around and recognized me immediately. "C-Weed!" I told him I needed a job. He replied, "Come see me at the legislature next week."

A few days later I received an official invitation from Eric's office. Meantime, I kept thinking, "What skills do I have? I've been running a band and writing songs all of my adult life." But Bryan drew up a list of what he called "deliverables," all the things I could do, such as helping organize the Junos and so on. I don't know how Bryan managed to figure out all these skills I possessed after playing in a band for twenty years. Like I've been saying, Bryan has always been my biggest fan and support. I miss that guy.

I met Eric in his big office in the Legislative building. We sat at a giant conference table and talked, the upshot being that he gave me a job. He didn't know what to do with me but said, "We'll have to find you a place." His staff found me an office in one of their buildings, gave me a computer that I didn't even know how to fire up, and a business card stating, "Music Consultant." The staff and the deputy Minister at the Arts Branch were most gracious to me for the time that I spent there. For the first month I spent my mornings at Garry's Deli in Winnipeg Square reading the newspaper. Derek would come by and we'd hang out there and visit.

Finally, Eric found a spot for me at MARIA (Manitoba Audio Recording Industry Association) over on Donald Street at Notre Dame, behind the Burton Cummings Theater. My role was to provide mentorship to Indigenous musicians navigating through the music business.

In my capacity as Indigenous music facilitator, I helped to create the annual Manito Ahbee Festival and the Aboriginal Peoples Choice Music Awards. But my first task was putting together the Indigenous music component of the 2005 Juno Awards celebrations in Winnipeg. CARAS (the Canadian Academy of Recording Arts & Sciences) was blown away by what I had organized to honour the five nominees in the Indigenous music category. The first three years of Manito Ahbee and the Aboriginal Peoples Choice Music Awards were terrific events celebrating various aspects of Indigenous culture and music. We used the Bell MTS Centre under the Community Use & Access program and in doing so fulfilled one of its obligations for being partially funded by the province. One year, Buffy Sainte-Marie was honoured for her dedication, contributions, and inspiration to Manitoba Indigenous artists. After the second year, the board of directors took control of the event and it was never the same, with government appointees and costs incurred for people who had no experience in the positions that they held. I was offered a chance to stay on with limited control and half the salary; I declined. I will be forever grateful to Culture Minister Eric Robinson for creating the opportunity for me to do all the things that I do best for those years of my life.

In spite of the rollercoaster ride of the previous decade, I hadn't abandoned music, or perhaps more significantly, music hadn't abandoned me. In 1988 I released *Tribute To Southern Rock* under the C-Weed name alone. Joining me on the CD were my brother Don, Clint and Tom Dutiaume, Gord Raffey, and Craig Fotheringham, who also produced the recordings. The songs were mostly cover songs by southern rockers including The Charlie Daniels Band, the Allman

Brothers, and Lynyrd Skynyrd, songs that had influenced me in the 70s plus one original song, "Old Rodeo Cowboys." We made a video for that one song. Former CBC radio host Ross Porter was working for the Cultural Industries Development Office (CIDO), which gave out government grants to artists. He got me the money to make the video. The album was released on my own Hawk Records. I signed other artists to Hawk Records, and for a time in the 1990s I was a record label operator.

Despite only one original song on the *Tribute To Southern Rock* project, I've always written songs and that had continued. I didn't perform as much or go out on the road for long stretches by then, but the desire to stand onstage before an audience was still strong. One of my finest compositions emerged at the start of a new decade.

It was back in 1990 when I was living on Burrows Avenue. I had been up all night and was sitting in front of the big picture window in my living room. I would compose something, then sing the song into a big JVC ghetto-blaster. I had just finished writing "I Wanna Fly" and I put the paper down. There was a crack in the curtain behind me and a beam of the morning light shone directly onto the paper. It was 5:30 in the morning and the sun was just coming up. It was one of those goosebump moments. I intuitively sensed that I had just written something special, something inspirational. It's about salvation and connecting to my spiritual self. I had never written anything like it before. It had the power to lift me up and put me down somewhere else, somewhere sober, clean and free.

I called my brother Stirling and told him I had to show him something. He said "Okay. Do you know what time it is?" and I replied "I do. Put some coffee on and I'll be right over." I drove over to his house on Inkster Boulevard, not that far. I walked in with the JVC blaster, sat down and played him the song from start to finish. He listened intently before saying, "Play it again." So, I did. He then asked to hear it a third time. Once it was done, he looked at me and said, "You've struck gold, boy!"

Singing "I Wanna Fly"

I Wanna Fly

Gonna lay my weight down at your feet
And rest here for a while
I'm feeling low Lord I feel defeat
Feel I've just walked my last mile
So I'll rest here for a while
I'm hiding from the street

I been to church Lord I've been to school
But I couldn't find you there
So I defied them I broke all their rules
I just didn't seem to care when I couldn't find you there
Oh Lord I've been a fool.

I wanna fly like a free bird flies
There's a blue sky calling me
Cause then I know that I'll always be
In the shelter of your smile you were with me all the while
Waiting patiently
Some call it karma
Some folks call it faith
They say one day you'll understand
But when you're down it's all one big mistake
Lord I finally understand you can take me by the hand
And lead me on your way
I wanna fly like a free bird flies
there's a blue sky calling me
'Cause then I know that I'll always be
In the shelter of your smile
You were with me all the while
Waiting patiently

I believed strongly in "I Wanna Fly" and I realized it was a turning point. My clean and sober life began, but at that time the original band had scattered. Everybody had moved on. I was nine months without a gig and I think I suffered the most in that time. Not so much from withdrawal from cocaine. I suffered from not being able to play. But "I Wanna Fly" renewed my confidence. As a result, I assembled a band, hired hands on salary, all great individual players in their own right: Randy Hiebert on guitar, Craig Fotheringham on keyboards, drummer Greg Black and Gord Raffey on bass guitar. We went into Dave Roman's Maddock Studio in Winnipeg and with Craig producing and Dave Roman engineering, we cut ten tracks, with a couple of collaborations with Craig and Randy (also one with Jimmy Flett) plus a cover of Trooper's "Janine" (I had the opportunity to sing that song with Trooper when they played at my club in Saskatoon and again in Winnipeg at the Pandora Inn). The resulting album was titled *I Wanna Fly* and was released as an Errol Ranville album, not the C-Weed Band.

There's a song of mine entitled "Oh Cocaine" on the album. That one came from my experience. "A taste of the fruit from the forbidden tree; I wanted the high that reached to the sky but, I never ever wanted to be there alone" Like Merle Haggard once said, "You've got no right to sing the blues unless you've had the blues" and I've certainly had 'em.

Entertainment lawyer David Wolinsky and Fred 'BTO' Turner had formed Thunder Records and I became their first signing with the *I Wanna Fly* album. David, Fred and their wives came to see me playing at my Winnipeg cabaret. I was very impressed by that. Clean and sober, they felt I was worth investing in. Unfortunately, the Thunder Records Label did not last long but I was able to retain the masters and later released *I Wanna Fly* on my own label.

When the album came out, I took the guys from the sessions out on the road. Greg Black was too busy with sessions and other work in the city, so Doug Yule joined on drums. We hit the road running.

All these guys were the cream of crop on the Winnipeg scene. You'd think, then, that together they would knock the doors off clubs. But in reality, it wasn't like playing with my brothers. It wasn't the same feeling for me. There wasn't the same camaraderie. We were billed as the C-Weed Band since, in the eyes and ears of the public, the C-Weed band was me and whomever was in the band at the time. But it didn't gel as a band. It wasn't a band of brothers, both figuratively and literally. They were hired guns.

I recorded *The Cowboy Code* album in 1995 with Craig Fotheringham and Tom Dutiaume playing multiple instruments along with Jason Chabluk on harmony vocals. The title song, "The Cowboy Code" remains one of my favourites. I really wanted to write a ballad, a cowboy ballad. The inspiration for that song came from the movie *Pat Garrett & Billy the Kid* that had Bob Dylan acting in it. I was moved by the story, so I wanted to write a song that told that story from Billy the Kid's point of view rather than Pat Garrett's. It's a good old-fashioned story song. When we recorded the album, Craig played the drum parts on a drum machine. I should have done more to promote the album after it was released because it's got some of my best songwriting. It's all original songs except for a cover of Neil Young's "Harvest." When Leslie left, I got into a real funk, so *The Cowboy Code* CDs sat piled up in my office at the cabaret. I put a great band of hired guns together once again with Tom Dutiaume on guitar and fiddle, Paul Hampton on the keyboards, Gord Raffey on bass guitar and Rod Demski on drums. We toured briefly but it wasn't nearly enough promotion for such a great project. We did get to play the US Indigenous Casinos over the border in Minnesota and South Dakota. That band was a lot of fun and we were playing all the songs off the *Cowboy Code* album in the live concerts. That CD should have done better but I was preoccupied with emotional survival and running the cabaret.

The Cowboy Code

When I close my eyes, I can see you in black
Riding tall holding on the reins
I can see the corral and the smoke from the shack
Where you'd go to heal your pain
The hole in the wall is still the same now
As back when you taught us all
To make retreat when we're feeling the load
Bill you taught us the Cowboy code
The cowboy code ain't written nowhere
You'll find it in your best friend
The outlaw outcast one who cares
And will ride with you till the end
A poet a gypsy a singer of songs
we've all been down that road
Grandpa said you never did no wrong
You lived by the Cowboy code
And we all know that you didn't run
When you split for New Mexico
Pat never would've got you Billy
You died for the Cowboy code
Pat never woulda got you Billy
You died for the Cowboy Code
The blood red sky is closing in
and the desert sand burns your feet

In the arms of love you're wondering why
it's cold and you feel defeat
Pat Garrett still fights in the dead of night
and to run he has to try
Before morning comes and all is done
Billy you'll have learned to fly

And we all know that you didn't run when you split for New Mexico
Pat never woulda got you Billy
You died for the Cowboy Code
Pat never woulda got you Billy
You died for the Cowboy Code
The famous final scene always brings a tear
it's a sorry tale to tale
How you turned your back without any fear
I can still see you when you fell
The heart decides and you can't pretend
each time a truth is born
Was it for Pat Garrett or you my friend?
in the end did people mourn
Sheriff Pat Garrett may you rot in hell
for selling out your best friend
This is a story I've had to tell
your spirit has no end
It still flows down that old Rio Grande
In the wind through New Mexico
And I'm feeling small try to make a stand
And live by the Cowboy Code
And we all knew that you didn't run
when you split for New Mexico

Pat never would've got you Billy
You died for the Cowboy Code
Pat never would've got you Billy
You died for the Cowboy Code

The Cowboy Code remains my favourite album that didn't sell. It also was released in 1995 under my own name, not the C-Weed Band. I love all those songs, but some people said it was too much like a Craig Fotheringham album. He played just about everything on it.

I realize now that he was exerting too much influence and control over the sessions and, thus, over me and my music. But I was busy with the club and just wanted to get an album out.

Sadly, Craig Fotheringham passed away in January 2012 of pancreatic cancer. He worked with many artists over the years and always brought his heart and soul to his music production. There is no denying his contributions to the success of The C-Weed Band.

I never listen to my own albums. I don't like listening to my music once it's been recorded. After all, I'm playing the songs every night so why would I then want to come home and listen to them? If I listen to music, I'll play the music I like: Merle Haggard, The Beatles or Jackson Browne. But the only album I ever listen to of my own music is *The Cowboy Code* album.

I released *I Wanna Fly* and *The Cowboy Code* under my own name. At that point I was looking to establish my own identity beyond the C-Weed Band. Many people in the music business didn't know that Errol Ranville was C-Weed, so it was helpful for me. This was my first foray into an independence from my brothers and operating my own career.

During the cabaret years, I recorded a couple of albums live at C-Weeds Cabaret backed by The Spirit River Band: guitarists Dennis Dick and Gerry McIvor, bassist Trevor Smith and Andy Dick on drums. These were a mix of well-known C-Weed Band songs and cover tunes. Dave Roman from Maddock Studios and a member of the D-Drifters engineered the albums from DAT tapes we recorded at the Winnipeg C-Weeds Cabaret.

I've had a history of dying and coming back to life again, figuratively speaking, falling and rising, resurrection and redemption. I've been doing it all my adult life and I'm still doing it. I'm a survivor. But that would be tested more than I or anyone could ever have imagined in the new millennium.

CHAPTER 5

On My Way Back Home

My son called me and when I answered the phone he blurted out, "Oh my god, am I ever glad to hear your voice!" Startled, I asked him why. He said, "I just heard on the radio that there's been a car accident on the way to The Pas and some of the C-Weed Band were killed! Have you heard from Uncle Errol?" I just went cold because I knew that Errol had been on his way to The Pas for the gig. —*Don Ranville*

When he arrived at the Health Sciences Centre in Winnipeg, I was standing there talking with the surgeon discussing Errol's leg and his life, what needed to be done. There were so many broken bones. And then I looked at Errol. I did not want to touch him anywhere because I didn't know what was broken. I looked at his hand lying there and there was no hair. Everything was burned off. He was red from first-degree burns and his hair was matted. There was soot and blood in his hair and on his face. He was kind of aware of us being there but not really. I was thinking, "Okay, at least he is awake." But I knew he was in shock and trauma. At that point I don't think he even remembered what had happened to him. I tried cleaning him

up, washing his face. The staff and surgeon were more concerned about his massive injuries. I didn't want to move him and I wasn't sure where to touch him. But I was just so relieved he was alive.
—*Roxanne Shuttleworth, niece*

I met Marcie Tyl Boles in January 2005 at an AA meeting. There was an instant connection between us. She did computer work for fashion design company Nygard International, owned by fashion mogul Peter Nygard, on Inkster Boulevard. She was well-organized and very good at her job. Marcie worked there for a number of years even after we got together. She was divorced from her husband, an ex-cop, and estranged from her three children who lived with the ex-husband. It was a very troubled situation. Her husband was a big man with a temper. She confided that she began to feel unsafe. It was at that point that she left him and left her kids. As a result, Marcie was also estranged from her parents and siblings who blamed her for the marriage falling apart. I was the one who picked her up off the figurative ground and put her back on her feet again. Her ex hated me for doing that but, strangely, he was afraid of me, a skinny little Neeche guy.

It was obvious right away that she completed me. I had never felt a level of trust, of bonding, that I felt with Marcie. I had never opened up to another person in my life until I was with her. I think that was the first time in my whole life that I actually learned how to treat a woman. It was quite a new experience for me. We were like soulmates, very close, closer than I had been with anyone in my life to that point. People who saw us together always commented on how we looked together, like we were in love. We were always holding onto each other, no matter when or where. She was the light that made me shine.

She was a joy. Our relationship was a joy. Marcie was so organized, and I just loved that about her. She had it together. She took over some of my projects and got things done. We were like two peas in the same pod. She wasn't Indigenous but that never mattered. All my siblings and associates loved her, too. She could be stubborn and stand her ground, but I respected her for that. She knew how to take care of me. We became inseparable. Because she travelled with me, everybody got to know her. She remembered everybody's name. She would have made a good politician.

When Marcie moved in with me, her parents were not pleased about it. She said they were racist and were against her being with an Indian. They pretty much cut her off when we married. I guess they were afraid of having to be around Indians.

We married in 2006 in a ceremony held at my son Derek's in-laws' restaurant, Gasthaus Gutenberger, on Portage Avenue in St. James, officiated by Eric Robinson. Of course, her parents did not attend. My daughter-in-law Sandra and my two grandchildren Brandan and Amber Sky were also in attendance, so it was a beautiful intimate occasion with my family. We later honeymooned in San Francisco.

I had been spending holidays in Mexico since 1988 with Leslie and continued to spend two weeks a year there for the next eighteen years. I loved Mexico and the first time I went to Huatulco with Marcie, she fell in love with the whole area around Huatulco. The next year we rented a beautiful place right on the ocean. It was idyllic. The second year we ended up purchasing the condo next door. We spent the next five years in our condo and got to know all the locals. I think one of the main reasons we enjoyed going back to Huatulco every year was for the people. They worked hard, didn't own anything but had a great sense of humour. We would stay in touch over the summer with the people who owned the shops downstairs. It would be so nice to arrive back in the fall just to see all the people again. In October 2010 we were wrapping up a series of gigs with the C-Weed Band and preparing to leave for Huatulco. We played in Marathon, Ontario, from there back to Goodfish Lake, Alberta, then back to Winnipeg, like that. We were going up to Opaskwayak Cree Nation in northern Manitoba. That would be our last show of the summer before Marcie and I left for Mexico.

Marcie and Errol

Marcie always wanted to own a Jeep. She picked one out from a photo in a flyer and had her heart set on it, it had to be that specific colour so I bought it for her. No one had ever done anything like that for her in her life. That was in July 2010. Marcie and I travelled together in her Jeep on those last tour dates before the accident. We were set to head up to The Pas. Marcie and I were travelling separate from the band and the equipment. We were looking forward to the gig because we were very popular in The Pas and had played there regularly over the years. The people of The Pas loved the C-Weed Band. We were booked to play the Aseneskak Casino. It was Thursday night, October 7. We were heading into the Canadian Thanksgiving long weekend.

I've been a working musician all my life. Part and parcel of that vocation is travel. You have to tour if you want to make a living. That's the reality. But the risks are there, and the more time you spend on the road, the greater the odds that something's going to go wrong. As The Band's Robbie Robertson said in their farewell concert film *The Last Waltz*, "The road has taken a lot of the great ones. You're pressing your luck after sixteen years. It's a goddamn impossible way of life." We had a near fatal crash on the road near Sudbury. We had two vans. I was driving the van in the lead when a car came careening towards me end over end. When I saw the car coming at us, I literally stood on the brakes applying my entire body weight. When the cops arrived on the scene, they had to pry my hands off the wheel. I was in a state of shock. I thought we were dead. All the gear was squished up against me, the guys driving the van behind me said they saw the tires smoking and catch fire but luckily went out right away. A close call.

The entertainment manager for the Aseneska Casino in Opaskwayak, Rhonda, had moved the gig date back a week from the 15th to the Thanksgiving long weekend. Marcie was somewhat upset about that because Thanksgiving weekend was a big deal for her. She spent that time with her kids and made a big meal. She wasn't happy that we had to go out of town that weekend. It was getting later and later that evening and I wanted to get there in sufficient time to catch some sleep and have a normal day on Friday, game day. I was trying to get her rolling. Finally, we got out the door. Max, my four-year-old Boxer dog, came with us. I later realized that Marcie had left her Macintosh computer at home on the kitchen counter. She always travelled with it, never without it. Except this time. A possible omen?

We arrived at the corner just before Grand Rapids to go down the Easterville Road, Highway 60 to connect up with Highway 10. We needed fuel. I thought we could get fuel in Easterville but as it turned out that little station was closed. We had to drive all the way back to Grand Rapids. I remember letting Max out to pee at Pelican Narrows gas bar. There was a couple there making a big fuss, "It's C-Weed!" (must be the black hat). She wanted a photo with us. Marcie was always so polite to anybody and everybody. I remember posing for a picture before we got back in the Jeep and on the road again.

It was well after midnight. Marcie and I were in her Jeep driving up Highway 10, which was partially under construction. I'd driven that highway dozens of times over the decades, but I never took highway travel for granted. We passed the trailer park just before the town of The Pas. I remember pointing it out to her as the first sign of life after a long, lonely stretch of road. The next thing I remember is seeing a light coming around the curve just before the Super 8 Motel. I couldn't make it out. It looked weird to me seeing this one small light all by itself. We said to each other, "What the hell is that?" I was just kicking off the cruise on the Jeep. In the next four or five seconds the strange light came up and over the incline. Turns out it was a driver's side running light. It was a car coming at us in the middle of the road. No headlights on. Suddenly Marcie screamed, "You're going too fast! They're in our lane!" That was it. There was no time to react.

I remember the thud. It was like "WHACK!" I didn't hear anything else. My memory is scattered after that. I can remember bits and pieces. I'm not sure what was real and what wasn't. I yelled at Marcie to get out of the car because I knew it was on fire. The fire and smoke actually woke me up. Then I looked over at her. To this day I wish I hadn't. The motor had been pushed right through her and all I could smell was burning flesh. The impact had killed her instantly. The dashboard had squashed up against my legs. I was stuck so I felt down to reach the lever under the seat. I hit the lever, the seat went back and freed my legs. But then I couldn't get the car door open. In my mind I saw my brother Gordon who had passed away a decade earlier helping me get out. Clearly that wasn't reality. I managed to crawl out and fell onto the road. I then walked around the Jeep and tried to open her door, but the plastic handle had melted. I looked down and my right foot was facing the wrong way, all twisted and facing backwards. I didn't really feel the pain until then. I fell backwards and rolled down into the ditch. I kept lifting my head up from the water. It's ironic because here I was surviving the crash only to drown in a ditch. Max, my dog, also died in the accident.

A passing truck driver stopped and ran over to the crash site. A second truck pulled up behind the first truck and the two drivers pulled me out of the water. They didn't want to move me fearing any further movement might cause greater injuries than I had already suffered so they lifted me very carefully. The Jeep burned for another half hour before it exploded. I felt the heat of the fire and heard the sound of the explosion but I didn't see it happen. All I knew was that Marcie was inside and I had been unable to save her. Not a good thought.

I could hear the two truck drivers talking. I couldn't talk. I had all the soot from the fire in my throat. I wanted to call out for them to save Marcie, but I couldn't talk. I could not remember that Marcie was already gone. I could hear all the confusion as I drifted in and out of consciousness. I don't know how long I was conscious. I did hear the police and ambulance sirens.

I know that another car came upon the scene from the direction of The Pas. It came screeching up to the two mangled vehicles then sped off South down Highway 10 towards Swan River. I don't know who was driving that car. Whoever sees this I guess will know that I know that a car came to the scene and left.

The next thing I remember was waking up in the Medevac airplane. I learned later that I had been ambulanced to The Pas hospital but they deemed my injuries so severe that I needed to be transported to Winnipeg. I screamed at the staff on the plane to get Marcie out of the car. I didn't know where I was, but I knew that Marcie was still in the car. Then one of the officers leaned over and said to me, "Your wife didn't make it." I stopped screaming. That's all that I remember of that part until I came to at the Health Sciences Centre. I vaguely remember being wheeled across the tarmac when we landed because it was really rough and painful. I remember talking to my brother Stirling who was the first to see me in the hospital. The doctors had told him that if I made it through the first forty-eight hours then I had a chance to live. It was pretty grim.

I was extremely lucky. When you look at the Jeep afterwards, the wreckage, and try to figure out my injuries, somehow, I got out of there alive, unlike the others. Yes, I suffered massive injuries, but

I survived. My right leg was crushed. Doctors worked twelve hours on it. They ended up putting a wheel in to replace my ankle because there was no ankle left. The surgeon showed me the x-ray of the wheel. It has about a 65% range of motion.

As for my left leg, the doctors said there were bones broken in a hundred places. My right leg was crushed. In my back, I had a cracked lumbar five. I couldn't move for the longest time because of my back. But the biggest trouble I had was my collapsed sternum. I had difficulty breathing. When the airbag activated it punched me like a sledgehammer to the chest. There is not much they could do for that. It had to heal on its own.

I continued to drift in and out of consciousness those first few days in hospital. I remember talking to family members but can't be sure what I was saying. I still didn't know all the details of the accident, but I was aware that Marcie had been killed. My niece Roxanne Shuttleworth, my older sister Valerie's daughter, was a life saver in those early days. I remember her cleaning up my face when I first arrived in the hospital. I had soot in my mouth and in my nose. She was there constantly. If I fell asleep, she would leave and most of the time when I would wake up, she would be at my bedside. I think I told her my life story, everything I ever felt or thought. I believed that if I kept talking like I did I wouldn't feel the effects of the depression. A lot of people came to see me. Among them were family members, White and Indigenous musicians, politicians and community leaders. Cultural Minister Eric Robinson, former Grand Chief of the Assembly of First Nations Phil Fontaine, Indigenous spirit leader Elijah Harper, who brought down both the provincial and federal governments with a feather. The members of Loverboy came by, too. They were playing a casino in town and doing a sound check at McPhillips Street Station. Spider has been a friend of mine for many years, and they came to cheer me up. We're all brothers of the road. No matter what genre of music we play, we all share the same experiences living on the road and they understand the risks we take while being on the road. The first couple of days in the hospital there were too many people there to visit me, over two hundred people in the hallways, clogging up the elevators. As a result, they moved me to another part of the hospital, and no one was given my room number anymore when they phoned the hospital. Roxanne became the gatekeeper. You can't really argue with her.

I fell into a deep depression while in hospital. When someone was depressed, I used to say, "Just pull up your socks and get at it. What is the matter with you? Shake it off." But then when I was there myself, I realized that I had no power; I was going down, like sinking into quicksand and I couldn't get out. And I remember thinking that this is what they were talking about when they were feeling depressed and shut down.

I spent sixty-six days in hospital recovering from injuries and operations. I remember thinking about Marcie and how she suffered spousal abuse and how her parents were against her marrying an Indian. Then I realized they couldn't hurt her anymore. No one could hurt her now. At that moment the dark cloud lifted from me, realizing she was in a safe place now.

Marcie's children came to see me in the beginning. I don't know what happened, but something caused a ruckus out in the hallway and they started fighting with Roxanne and my sister Delphine. It became loud and ugly, nasty words thrown back and forth. I couldn't get involved because I had to watch my heart rate. I thought I was going to explode. They were yelling and screaming, and my heart was going too fast, four times my normal rate. I called an orderly. I had to leave the fury out in the hallway. I couldn't deal with it at that moment. I was just trying hard to focus on the business of staying alive.

I never saw nor heard from them again. As it turned out, Marcie's family wanted to have a funeral as fast as possible, while I was still in the hospital. And my siblings were telling them no. Everyone was saying to me that Marcie's family just wanted to have a funeral quickly so that there'd be no Indians there. I refused, saying, "We'll have a funeral when I can go to it. Right now, I can't, I can't sit up, I can't get up. I cannot attend a funeral." I knew that racism was present in Marcie's family and I knew that was why she was alienated from her parents and siblings. Her parents, sister and brother had not spoken to her in ten years. I can't imagine that kind of situation. I do know that it broke Marcie's heart. I was with Marcie for almost eight years and I finally met her dad at the gravesite. That was the first time I met the guy. For her to marry an Indian was the ultimate disgrace as far as that family was concerned. And as it turned out, when the funeral was eventually held in May 2011, there were like 500 people attending and probably 400 of them were Indigenous, people who loved me and loved Marcie.

It was in the hospital that I learned the details of the accident. It literally all happened in a matter of seconds. There were four teenagers, ages fifteen to sixteen, Indigenous kids, who had been drinking Thursday evening at a beer bash at University College of the North. They were underage but managed to acquire alcohol. I think the College allowed underage kids to drink there, justifying it as better to have them drink there where they could watch them and keep them off the streets. Except they didn't do that on this night. Somehow the kids, at this point there were five of them, left the beer bash drunk and got into a 1998 Chevrolet Cavalier. They drove down the street sideswiping cars, drove right past the RCMP detachment to McDonald's. They stopped at the McDonald's and raised hell there. Noisy, loud and disruptive. Drunk. They got back in the car but one of them jumped out. They ditched him there. He's still alive in The Pas. The four in the Chevy Cavalier—Nicole Jean Rabiscah-Hill, Jessica Dorion, Dion Constant and Ken Lathlin Jr.—ended up on the main highway, playing chicken with passing motorists. No headlights on, swerving all over the road. It was approximately 4:30 in the morning, Friday October 8 when they came around the curve just south of The Pas, left their side of the highway and drove straight into our Jeep head on. They were killed instantly as were Marcie and

Max, our dog. The blood alcohol count on all four teenagers was .248, three times over the legal limit. I have since spoken with a medical expert who told me that with that amount of alcohol in their system, they should have been unconscious.

When there is a fatality on a Manitoba highway, a forensic crew from the Manitoba government is always dispatched to go to the accident site. There were five fatalities that night. However, on this occasion those experts were not dispatched. The RCMP closed off the highway at the scene and one of their own constables was the one who did the highway forensics. Much of the details came from the surviving kid who got out at McDonald's. My late friend Arnold Constant raised this boy. Arnold and his wife went and got him right away, brought him back to their house, and made him explain what had happened. The kid then related the details to the local RCMP. It seemed like a clear, open and shut case: the teenagers were fully intoxicated and in the wrong and no one had done anything to stop the chain of events that culminated in the tragic accident. But there were local and provincial parties who were very concerned about liability for the accident and they were determined to blame it on me.

I came home two weeks before Christmas, December 12, 2010, still confined to a wheelchair. The quiet in the house was deafening. It was hard to be alone. My younger sister Donna stayed with me for a while before returning to Toronto, where she lived at the time. I didn't know whether I had a future or what I would do. It was many months of being dysfunctional and not even being able to go out of the house. The grieving and recovery were a challenge. But I never considered turning to alcohol or drugs to try to heal the pain. Never did. It would have been easy to do, and I'm sure there were people who would have forgiven me if I had, but I knew I couldn't do it. I had too much invested personally in my sobriety to turn my back on it. My friend Ray T. picked me up in my wheelchair and brought me to AA meetings during this time.

The house was so quiet, so empty, and I felt so alone. That was the hardest thing to deal with, the loneliness. On the other hand, I needed that silence. I didn't even pick up a guitar much. I thought my career was over, my life was over. I had never been sensitive to depression but once I had a taste of it, I understood how people could not function while depressed. It's completely debilitating, overwhelming. I spent the better part of a year after the crash in a deep depression. I didn't start to heal until I picked up a guitar and a pen. I started writing all the songs for the *Forever* album. I wrote all twelve songs on the album. Just getting back to writing again, I knew that I was whole again. I was functioning and I was going to be okay.

Meantime, the investigation remained open for a year. It appeared obvious what had happened; the four kids were driving recklessly and drunk and ploughed into Marcie and me. However, that's not how the RCMP reported it. I woke up one morning and found all of these messages on my phone. The first call I took was from Eric Robinson who asked me if I had seen the morning newspaper. I said no. I went to the front door to get the *Winnipeg Free Press*. Sure enough, there was a big article on page two: "Local musician charged." The newspaper article said that, after long and hard deliberation, the RCMP detachment in The Pas (the same detachment that had oversight over the Helen Betty Osborne murder) in conjunction with Manitoba Justice had decided to charge me. With all that liability, I think the authorities in the justice system wanted to make it all go away by charging me with careless driving. Not even careless driving causing death, just careless driving. They were assuming that the charge and threat of prison would be enough to scare me into pleading guilty and then everybody would be off the hook. It is only careless driving, after all. Let the Neeche guy take the fall. He won't fight it. The whole horrific incident came back to life for me and, worse yet, for the families of the four kids.

On the recommendation of a friend, I retained a lawyer (who shall remain nameless) to fight my case in court, a high-profile, well-established, well-respected family firm of father and son. The father, who graduated from law school in 1957, had a long and eminent career as a defence attorney while the son handled malpractice litigations. The father served as my attorney along with an associate from the firm. The two seemed determined to make everyone happy and settle this quickly. That seemed to be their only strategy. To that end they attempted to convince me to plead out. Take a guilty plea and the worst I would get is a fine and temporary loss of my driver's license. Easy peasy. The two of them worked on me all morning and I was paying $240 per hour between the two of them. They explained to me over and over again that if I pleaded guilty, I wouldn't have to go to court. I was likely looking at a $5,000 fine and a five-year suspension of my license with no jail time. If I went to court it was going to cost me $50,000. I would have to mortgage my house just to pay their legal fees. To them, a guilty plea made logical and expedient sense and most of all would establish liability.

Except, I kept insisting, I was not guilty. I hadn't done anything wrong. I hadn't committed a crime. They were persistent and kept at me.

Finally, I called Eric Robinson to asked him for advice. He told me he couldn't tell me what to do. I had to decide for myself what I was going to do. He did say, though, that if I knew I hadn't done anything wrong, I shouldn't plead guilty. But in the end, I signed their paper. They waved that paper in my face for three hours. I went home. That was a rough, sleepless night.

At 7:30 the following morning I was on the phone to the lawyers' office. No answer. Finally, at 8:30, I got the father on the line. I said I needed to get that paper back. "I'm not pleading guilty to something that I'm not guilty of." "I guess we are going to have to go to court," was his response, followed by, "Have you got $50,000?" They needed to know I could afford to proceed with a court battle. I said, "Well, I'll have to try and get it. How about if I give you $30,000?" "We can start with that." Now they had to start building the case.

The RCMP maintained that somehow or other I lost control of my vehicle, crossed the line between the two highways, and slammed into the Cavalier killing the four kids. They said that they could prove that I fell asleep at the wheel and lost control, and as a result, I went over into their oncoming lane and hit their car. Because my car, the Jeep, was so much heavier, it pushed the kids' car back ending up perfectly back in my lane. Two cars defying the law of physics like that. They claimed the skid marks showed the car was pushed back. They had a sketch of the accident site, a pencil drawing. How they came to that conclusion I have no idea since the crash site and the positioning of the two vehicles did not support their theory in any way. The RCMP did not once consider that another car coming from the direction of The Pas skidded to a stop alongside the crash site and then sped off heading south down highway 10. They instead claimed that the skid marks were from the Cavalier that the four teenagers were driving. I realized it was going to be a tough fight.

Among the flaws in their assertion was the damage to our Jeep. The damage is on an angle. The Cavalier hit our vehicle head-on with the majority of the impact to the passenger front side where Marcie was. The Cavalier pushed in that side of the Jeep.

My lawyer told me we needed to get a reconstructionist, someone who reconstructs the accident for the court case. He got his friend, ex-RCMP, to do the reconstruction. I guess he used him all the time. It cost me $6,000 for him to concur with the RCMP. Really? So now my case is even worse. I had paid an ex-RCMP officer to say that the current RCMP officer's forensics were against me. I could have saved myself $6,000. Back to the drawing board.

My lawyer then said he had a guy from Toronto who did highway forensics. That is all he does, reconstructing accidents on the 401 freeway in Toronto all day long. Another $9,000. Bob Shirer, my reconstructionist, tried to get all the photos taken at the scene of the accident as they are numbered in sequence but soon realized the RCMP only gave him 40% of the file. How was he supposed to do an accurate reconstruction with that? The RCMP wouldn't release all the photos. He tried for three months. They refused to release them. So, he did his reconstruction based on the amount of the file he was given access to. Even based on the limited information he was provided with, he was able to demonstrate that according to the laws of physics it was impossible for this accident to happen the way that the RCMP claimed it had. He also noted in his report that nobody had spoken to me, the accused, about specific details. The RCMP investigators had made up their own minds about what happened that night. The reconstructionist asked why I hadn't been asked in the RCMP interview about specifics, or believed when I said I could not remember certain details because of trauma?

The crux of the RCMP case rested on the assumption that I had fallen asleep at the wheel. That must be what happened they said. That's the only way they could make their conclusion work and lay the liability on me, charging me with careless driving by falling asleep while driving. After all, it was 4:30 in the morning when the accident took place. What about the negligence of UCN? What about the RCMP negligence? Were the RCMP liable because they failed to notice and stop these kids as they careened through town right past their offices and failed to attend to the ruckus the kids raised at McDonald's? The sentiment of the community was "How could the four teens from our community here in The Pas be responsible for such a dreadful tragedy?" It had to have been the outsider. I was being railroaded right from the time the RCMP dragged me off the highway.

In the end, I had to get my personal doctor to make a sworn statement that he has been treating me for insomnia for several years and that I could not have fallen asleep at the wheel. That blew a big hole in the RCMP's case. Then one of the truck drivers who happened upon the crash scene made a deathbed testimonial to my lawyer about what he witnessed and overheard between the RCMP officers on the scene that night. The truck driver had no agenda and no axe to grind. He was dying of cancer. He knew I was being railroaded and was so upset about that. He testified under oath that one of the cops that he was talking to was saying that these Indian kids like to drink a lot and it was hard to keep them off the highway in this condition. He observed that when the RCMP came on the scene they simply grabbed me by the scruff of the neck and dragged me onto the road and dropped me there on the pavement after the two truck drivers had been so careful in moving me out of the water in the ditch. The truck driver said the RCMP appeared to exhibit a negative attitude towards me because I was Indigenous.

The doctor's statement in the form of a letter was the clincher. I did not fall asleep at the wheel, and it is common for trauma victims to experience temporary amnesia or never remember at all what happened. That was their whole case, that Mr. Ranville fell asleep at the wheel and in doing so caused the accident. The RCMP claimed that I did not remember the accident because I had fallen asleep, but my doctor's letter stated that he had been treating me for chronic insomnia for fifteen years. I am not going to be able to fall asleep without my medication the doctor acclaimed in his letter. What the RCMP was claiming was preposterous. Why would I take pills if I was driving? Based on my doctor's letter, in late November 2012, the provincial court stayed the charges against me.

Having a stay of proceedings in the case left me in limbo. All it means is that the Crown or prosecution has chosen not to proceed further with the case at this point. It doesn't mean I'm acquitted or innocent. The case could be reactivated at any time up to one year. So where do I stand? I'm still not cleared. It's frustrating. I devoted over two years to the case and tens of thousands of dollars only to be left hanging. It's a no-win situation. Of course, the Crown cannot ever resurrect my case now that their one year window has elapsed, but I would like to be exonerated. To leave it this way satisfies only them. Five people died. Somebody has to be held responsible. We, the four families of the teens in The Pas and me, are all left to live with it, an unresolved situation. The truth is absolute. It is the one thing that remains constant and unchanged. You can do all the little diagrams and bullshit and deny my reconstructionist all of the file to work with to resolve the case, but all of these little interferences cannot change the truth. The fact of the matter is I am the only one living on this earth that was there, that can bear witness to what really and truly happened. If you want to know, ask me. I'll tell you. If you don't want to know the truth, then don't ask me. Like my reconstructionist said, "You guys have not even paid any attention to what Mr. Ranville has to say."

I was prepared to file a lawsuit against the liable parties involved: the people that provided the beer to the teens, the police detachment that was supposed to be on duty, the Manitoba Highways Department that left the highway in such dangerous condition overnight. The highway was not even finished. It was two levels and there were no markers. I was ready to sue and had been working with a Toronto law firm. They reviewed my case files and assured me that I had a strong case for damages in the millions of dollars. Two years later, after waiting for them to proceed with the suit, they suddenly told me they couldn't represent me because they couldn't secure an agent in Manitoba to act on our behalf. In their letter they urged me not to bother trying to sue the province and the RCMP. However, I'm not ruling out a suit one day.

To add further insult to injury, I had to fight with MPI, Manitoba Public Insurance or Autopac, over my insurance claim from the accident. If it had been a private insurance company, what happened to me in this accident, besides losing my wife and my dog, and the injuries that I sustained, the pain and suffering, and specifically the post-traumatic stress disorder, the payout would be in the tens of millions. I paid for that insurance all my adult life as a driver. My ability to tour extensively, even to be able to stand onstage for a full evening's show has been limited by the accident. My future income has been affected. I used to do thirty-five to forty shows a year, tour for months at a time, making X number of dollars. I cannot do that anymore. It is physically impossible.

Yes, I can go out and play a concert. I can get up and do certain things. I can't walk a long distance. I rely on a cane. But it's a hell of a lot better than sitting depressed in my house with the windows closed, the curtains drawn, and phone off the hook feeling sorry for myself. But MPI views everything I do from a position of mistrust. I haven't done anything wrong and yet I feel like I'm being punished. Bottom line, I am just trying to deal with what I have coming to me. I'm entitled to that insurance, yet they make me feel like a welfare cheat. I have to live every day under threat that MPI is going to pull the rug out from under me. My MPI file remains open.

In 2018, I returned to the site of the accident near The Pas. There are four homemade crosses in the ditch for the four teens. And a single cross with 'Marcie' written on it. The visit was for the documentary *The Road To Here: The Errol Ranville Story,* produced by my good friend Gary Zubeck and directed by Kevin Nikkel and Hanwakan Whitecloud. It was difficult standing on the spot where five people, including my wife, died. Regrettably, there are people in the community who bought into the contrived RCMP story and still believe I'm to blame. The charges by the RCMP and Manitoba Justice, even though they have been proven wrong, still put an ounce of doubt into the minds of the broken families. It remains a cruel and unusual punishment to us all in our community. There has been no reconciliation between me and the four families from Opaskwayak Cree Nation. That remains painful for me.

CHAPTER 6

Run As One

A year after the accident happened, Errol received the Lifetime Achievement Award at the Aboriginal Peoples Music Choice Awards. It was quite an emotional moment seeing him make his way onstage to the podium with the aid of a cane. He had suffered incredible loss along with accusations, finger-pointing and confusion along with misrepresentations of what had really happened. He carried the weight of all that and still does. It's not easy. But it was like his purpose here on earth wasn't done yet. He still had work to do. And he went on to put the band back together, tour, write and record new songs, and mentor young artists. He patched up some old wounds. —*David McLeod, Executive Director, NCI (Native Communications Incorporated)*

Did the accident change Errol? I didn't notice. He was still a go-getter, always moving. He may have changed inside. I can't imagine it not changing him inside. —*Don Ranville*

In February 1997, the band travelled to Europe for gigs in Switzerland, Austria, Germany and the south of France. The response to our music was incredible. They really appreciate Indigenous artists over there and don't have any of the prejudices that exist back here. We even appeared on Swiss television. People over there have a very romantic vision of Indigenous people. Other Indigenous artists have experienced the same warm and welcoming response. They value our culture and anything that is authentically North American Indigenous. They understand our sense of identity and realize the value that we have as Indigenous people, the first people of North America. They respect our dignity and culture. We brought along some dreamcatchers and these people in Europe couldn't buy them fast enough and for big money. They only wanted to confirm that these cultural items were authentically made by an Indigenous person.

In November 2004, the C-Weed Band went to south central China to perform representing Canada at the Nanning International Folk Song Arts Festival. We were sponsored by the Chinese Embassy out of Vancouver. To them we were the true definition of Canadian music. They knew nothing about Indigenous culture in China. It was all new to them. The reality is that there is no stereotypical image of Canadian culture around the world. When you say Ukraine, you envision the colourfully dressed Cossack dancers and Ukrainian food. Same thing with Ireland or Spain or Italy. But we don't have any instantly recognizable identity as Canadians, except for hockey. Everything else in Canada came from somewhere else. So, there we were representing Canada with the Indigenous culture and music. And they loved us everywhere we played. At one venue, a university, we performed before 60,000 people. We were chaperoned everywhere by military personnel. In rural areas the people had never seen foreigners before and the first foreigners they were introduced to were Indigenous musicians.

When I think back on playing in Europe and China, I have to scratch my head and wonder how the hell these Neeche kids from

Eddystone, Manitoba made it to the world stage. They were playing our records on the radio in Switzerland and watching our live concert on Swiss TV.

Throughout the band's career, we never rode on our Indigenous coattails. We never waved the Indian flag. We never wanted to do that. The C-Weed Band opened the doors for other Indigenous artists. We broke trail for all those who have since followed. We created the circuit on reserves. We were also on mainstream radio and we weren't identified on air as being an Indian band. Strangely, a lot of people thought we were from the Maritimes. We were not trying to draw attention to Indigenous issues. Until "Run As One."

"Run As One" stands apart from all my other songs. I wrote it back in 1990 when the Oka uprising in Quebec was happening and gave it to Craig Fotheringham during the recording of *The Cowboy Code* album. His response was to save it for a later project, not now and not on this album. MLA Elijah Harper came to see me at C-Weeds Cabaret one night in 1990. He was going to Oka and he came to ask for my advice. We always shared our thoughts on politics and community. We sat together and talked about what was going on there and across Canada with Indigenous people. After he left, I wrote the song "Run As One."

Run As One

Held my tongue in a code of silence
Assessed the worth of the Oka violence
It's been a fight for what is right
Ancient treaties denied

1990 called it Indian summer
You could feel the beat of a distant drummer
So strong with pride side by side
We shared a social changing tide

We got to Run as One now its begun
feel the beat of a distant drum
close our ranks and give our thanks
to the spirit up above

It's our children's children I'm thinking of
They got to know they can rise above
100 years of quiet fear
And press for the mark
We got to Run as One now that its begun...

By that point I was releasing albums every five years or so. *The Cowboy Code* was released in 1995. By 2000 I was living in Edmonton running the club. I didn't have a band. I would sit in with bands playing at the club. My brother Don's son and my nephew Mike Bruyere showed up one day in Edmonton in a beat-up Ford Focus with his drums in the back and said to me, "You need to be playing, Uncle Errol. Let's start a band." So we brought in some guys from Saskatchewan to join us, Mitch Daigneault, Jay Ross, Elvis Ballentyne, Cornelius "Corny" Michelle, and later Rick Shott from Edmonton.

I waited for the Indigenous community to catch up. The song had a powerful unifying message that speaks to Indigenous people everywhere. It's an anthem. They weren't ready for "Run As One" in 1990. 1995? Not yet. In 2000 I had my ear to the ground and the time was right for that song. It was time to release it.

Everything evolves. Nothing stays the same. Every year there is a general assembly of Chiefs in Ottawa where different issues are shared and discussed. I have attended many of them. It is difficult to explain the read of the land or the pulse of a Nation. It's hard to give away your secrets when it is still somewhat of a secret to yourself. I sensed that the nations North, South, East and West were uniting on several fronts like never before. There was consensus that became valued. There was also a surge in the popularity of the powwows and a merging with mainstream events that gave a song like "Run As One" a window. Many said that the song came along at exactly the right time. Little did they know that I was waiting for exactly the right time to release it.

I wanted traditional singers on it. I know some bands use a bunch of white guys singing traditional chants, but I wanted the real thing. I have too much respect for traditional singers to fake it. We began recording at a small studio called The Recording Studio owned by a gentle soul, Frankie. We began calling him the nicest guy in the world, which he was. At that point I needed traditional singers. I was playing in Saskatoon at my night club and was talking to Julie Greyeyes, a schoolteacher, on our break. I told her about the song and that I needed a drum group with powwow singers. She replied that she knew who to approach, renowned traditional singer Edmund Bull, leader of the Red Bull Singers. She then said, "He's standing right over there, the guy with the ponytail." I went over and tapped Edmund Bull on the shoulder and introduced myself. I asked if he would like to sing on my next album and he replied "Yeah, it would be an honour." Just like that, right then and there, no hesitation. It was already a done deal. Edmund received approval from his Elders, and we were ready to go.

The Red Bull singers all arrived at Edmonton in a pickup truck. They were all very humble. They had a baby with them; I wonder where that baby is now. The baby was crawling around on the studio floor. They brought in the big drum and unwrapped it like they were unwrapping gold. They had great respect for the big drum. It was quite awe inspiring to watch.

The night before, they asked what I wanted them to sing. I don't write sheet music. All I could do was give them a tape of the song as it was so far. What are we doing? "Here's the beat, here's the key." They took it with them to the hotel. The next day they came to the studio and recorded the song in two takes. Mike Bruyere, my nephew, who also composed the song's catchy guitar riff, helped them find the beat. There was initially a problem with getting the timing right, the drum and the recorded track. I suggested they do the chant without the drum, but they said they couldn't do that. In the end Mike played the drum beat and they were able to sing the honour song while he played. It was very moving and so dramatic. We were listening back and, holy man, I will never forget it. The hair on the back of my neck was standing up when I listened to it. I had tears in my eyes. It was such an emotional moment for me hearing the authentic traditional chanting. One of those magical moments in my life. When Edmund finished singing the song solo, without the rest of the singers.

They appeared and disappeared from my life, just like that. But they changed me, just meeting them, hearing them, spending that time in their humble company and having them grace my song.

To this day, "Run As One" outsells all the C-Weed albums put together. It's huge and it's worldwide. It speaks to people in a way no other of my songs do. I never anticipated how much that song would resonate with a wider audience. It became a #1 song on radio for seventeen weeks. "Run As One" was nominated for a Juno award. We did not win but that is okay, we didn't need to. Just writing and recording that song, I had already won. I didn't need a Juno award to validate the power and the reach of the song across Canada. "Run As One" was a significant event for me as well as the for the Indigenous community because I included Edmund Bull and the Red Bull singers in the traditional honour song that leads into the lyrics that I wrote. The song became an anthem, a rallying cry across Turtle Island.

Ali Fontaine was a young Anishinaabe singer/songwriter from the Sagkeeng First Nation in Manitoba. Her father, Wayne Fontaine, and his wife Carol approached me about mentoring their daughter's singing career. I was moved by the story of Ali's talent and impressed when I heard her singing. She had been writing her own songs since she was fourteen years old (she was still in her teens when I first met her). She had good songs, good looks, a great voice and determination. It was early summer 2011 and I agreed to work with her. It was good for me because I was still recovering and struggling to walk, relying on a wheelchair from time to time. Ali helped my return to music by giving me a purpose and a focus. She came with me to New York and performed at the World Indigenous Business Forum.

I produced Ali's self-titled debut album with Tom Dutiaume at his recording studio. It was funny because both Ali and I were nominated for Native American Music Awards in 2012. We attended the ceremonies in Niagara Falls, New York. She won best country album and I did not. Maybe I am a better manager than I am an artist. I also produced her second album, *Diamond In The Rough*, which was a bit rockier. I worked with all aspects of promoting and managing Ali's career for two years. I brought her up to a level that she now could make money with her music for years into her future.

Ali went on to win the Aboriginal Peoples Choice Music Award for Most Outstanding Manitoban in 2011 and Female Entertainer of the Year in 2012. She has released three albums as of this writing and continues to pursue a music career while simultaneously furthering her education, working on her master's degree studying Indigenous culture.

I didn't date any other women for a long time after Marcie died. I was still grieving. I went to the medicine man and he told me that grieving was a real thing. A real emotion and experience. You cannot escape grieving and you should not be in such a panic about it. Embrace it, he said, because it is your doorway to recovery. You have to go through the grieving process before you can heal. He asked me exactly when the accident happened. And I told him October 8, 2010. He said, "Okay, so now it's early spring." It was in March. "You have gone through the winter and you have missed her. You will go through the spring and you will think of all the things you did together with her at this time of the year. The leaves are budding, the grass is starting to come alive. The summer will pass, and you will think of all the things you did with her the summers that you were with her. And then again in the fall. After a year if you are still grieving, then it is on you. You are just holding on to it." He said one year, that's it. You will have lived through each season since she has gone away and grieved for all that you have missed from the seasons that you had spent with her. It's time to move on.

I met Ashley Klassen a year to the day of the car crash. And on October 10, 2011 I asked her out. When Ashley came into my life, I was a year out of trying to survive. She came along and we became friends. Ashley was a tremendously gifted singer. I asked her to be a contestant at a Manitoba Star Attractions showcase that I was managing at the time.

When I saw her singing, I felt a connection right away. My niece Roxanne Shuttleworth was there, too, and she witnessed that connection. Ashley was twenty-four years of age, tall, slender with long curly blond hair, reminiscent of Marcie. I was narrowing in on 60. The age gap was a concern, but she said it's just a number, and not to worry about it. She sang backup on the *Forever* album, my return to music after the long darkness of depression and recovery and co-wrote the song "Walk Me to the Edge." The songs on the album were partly written for Marcie and partly for Ashley. She performed with the band once I started playing gigs again.

I invited Ashley to come to New York with me. I was playing a show there. This was early on in our relationship. She thought I was moving too fast, but I told her she would have her own room and her privacy. We'd just hang out together and get to know each other. She agreed to join me. We did everything. I rented one of those executive town cars at $900 per day. She could not believe it. We enjoyed a sunset boat cruise when all the lights come on in all the big buildings of The Big Apple. What a blast. We did the Empire State Building, the Statue of Liberty, I took her to see an opera at the Metropolitan Opera House. (Ashley is an opera singer.) It was a whirlwind trip.

She later paid me back with a dream trip of my own. I had told Ashley that I didn't attend many concerts, but there were two recording artists, long-time heroes and inspirations of mine, that I would dearly love to see. As it turned out, one of them, Bonnie Raitt, came to perform at the Winnipeg Folk Festival. We sat in the front row. It was a wonderful musical experience watching and listening to Bonnie perform. My other hero was Jackson Browne, whose songwriting had inspired me for decades. I even recorded two of his songs, "Black And White" and "For America" on my *Redemption* album.

Ashley surprised me with tickets to see Jackson Browne opening for another of my early rock music inspirations, John Fogerty of Creedence Clearwater Revival at the Jones Beach Amphitheater on Long Island, New York on August 5, 2014. What a concert experience! I was so pumped afterwards that I phoned my brothers Don and Wally and told them excitedly, "We have to make an album together again!" And I wrote "Last Ride" right there in my seat at the show, the whole song.

Ashley and I enjoyed a wonderful four years together. When it came time for her to leave, she didn't want anything from me. She wanted to make her own success in the world. "You supported me for four years, now it's time for me to try it on my own." I couldn't argue with that. Even though she is no longer with me anymore I love her to death. Ashley represented everything that was good and right. I think the time we spent together gave me the time I needed to get my feet back under me. She is doing very well in pursuit of her own dream these days.

After the accident, I was down on the touring part having to get out there where I might be vulnerable on the highways. Plus, all the hours at night trying to deliver my music live. I thought maybe I couldn't do that part anymore, but I could still write and record. Both Ali and Ashley brought me back into music, into being productive again, and feeling like I had something to contribute. It was a turning point for me. I felt useful again.

In 2011, I was honoured with the Lifetime Achievement Award at the Aboriginal Peoples Choice Music Awards celebrating my accomplishments thus far. I was still unsteady on my feet and relying on a cane. "It's kind of funny me receiving a lifetime achievement award," I remember saying to the audience in my acceptance speech. "I'm not done yet."

CHAPTER 7

Redemption

Errol is still carrying a flame and has a spirit ignited by music and working with people. That is something truly inspiring. There are so many people that we've lost along the way. We need people who can show us that glimmer of hope and tenacity and Errol has done that and continues to do so. That's why he is held in such high esteem. He's one of the last men standing who we have to be thankful for. He hasn't been perfect, he's made mistakes, and he knows that, but it makes him more human and maybe, in essence, makes it more allowable to learn from him. He has integrity. He has not lost that vision, that sense of "I am here to work with other people and show our best." Errol's legacy is about the possibility.—*David McLeod, Executive Director, NCI (Native Communications Incorporated)*

Errol has always mentored, always thought about the next, the ones coming. I don't know if that was taught, if it was something he learned, or if it was just part of who we are as Indigenous people. Because everything we do is about 'How is this going to affect the kids? How is this going to affect my grandchildren?' How is it going to affect the future ones coming up? Errol has always been like that, or thought like that, trying to make the road easier for those coming behind him.—*Roxanne Shuttleworth, niece*

I released the album *Hey* in 2006, taking the six tracks from my 2000 *Run As One* CD and adding five new songs recorded with Jesse Green (Billy Joe's son and a talented guitar player in his own right). The *Redemption* album was recorded in 2008 with Tom Dutiaume and Paul Hampton. The title song was my take on the state of Indigenous affairs since "Run As One" and the start of the Truth and Reconciliation hearings. The situation was progressing. That pendulum was beginning to swing. It's moving along. There is greater awareness of Indigenous issues and a lot of us have to find our place. There is a time for the fight, and I want to be part of the fight. I am in a position where I get to see and observe what works. We have seen a lot of the truth in the past five years and a lot of it has been recorded. I don't know what the Truth and Reconciliation Committee are going to do with those recordings. People came forward and spoke on the condition that they remain anonymous. But where is the reconciliation?

Redemption

They silenced the drum and songs we sung before I was born
Felt the weight come down on me, when I spoke in my own tongue
Feels like there's someone watching me, there's ghosts in these walls
Feels like I've been here before and it makes my skin crawl
It's time to tell our story for the whole world to see
It's time to teach our children and rewrite history
100 years, a thousand tears, complete humiliation
One man speaks after all these years for truth and reconciliation
A new day dawn, a brand-new world, sweet taste of redemption
Run as one, sound the drum for a nation within a nation
It's time to tell our story for the whole world to see
It's time to teach our children and rewrite history

The album also included my take on a John Fogerty track, "Déjà vu (All Over Again)" as well as an interpretation of David Bowie's "Heroes" that surprised a few people. Along with 2012's *Forever*, recorded after my accident, these albums put me back in the game.

A few months before the accident I had compiled a 'Best Of' kind of album including all the C-Weed Band's biggest hits, from "Evangeline" to "Redemption." Jesse Green remastered the tracks. When you listen to that CD from start to finish you really get a sense of how we developed as a band and evolved our sound. It's quite a body of work, but I wasn't finished yet. The photo on the CD cover is of Don and I only. It should have included Wally, too, since he played on just about every song on the album. But he wasn't back in the band yet.

One of Marcie's goals had been for me to get together with my brothers, Don and Wally and record again. She would say to me, "You need to get the C-Weed Band back together." Don had remained with me on and off for more than forty years, but I hadn't worked with Wally for almost three decades. We had some differences that had not been resolved. He's my brother and I'll always love him and will always acknowledge his contributions to the C-Weed Band. But we went our separate ways in the late 1980s. In fact, the four of us—me, Don, Wally, and Clint—hadn't played together as a band for twenty-eight years. Wally ended up on the outside looking in for all those years, but it was his choice. He never came to China with Don and me, and didn't come to Europe either. I always wished he could have been there with us as he was so instrumental in starting the band and helping me with the music.

Years later, Wally had borrowed some money from me for a business venture that didn't pan out for him. He had no way of paying me back but I was okay with that. Then around 2016, John Ervin, who had been playing bass for me live, couldn't make a gig. Don said to me, "Why don't you call Wally?" He came and played with us for that gig and it just felt right, the three brothers together again. After the gig, Wally didn't want any money. He wanted me to put it towards what he owed me. As it turned out, John Ervin lost his gig with the band

Don, Wally, me, and Clint outside the recording studio

as I kept calling Wally to play the live gigs so that he could pay off his debt to me. With Clint back in the fold, the C-Weed Band was back together. For me it was reassuring to look around me onstage and see my brothers with me again. It's come full circle. Here we are, twenty-eight years later, in our sixties playing together again and it feels so good, so natural.

With "Last Ride" as the catalyst and Paul Hampton assisting on keyboards, Don, Wally, Clint and I began recording at my home studio with Paul engineering the sessions. Everything came together like magic. The camaraderie was just like the good old days and the sessions were fun filled. Besides "Last Ride" I had seven more new songs written for the album and we rounded it out with a cover of The Band's "The Shape I'm In" written by Robbie Robertson, which became the number one song on the Indigenous Music Countdown. It happens that some forty years ago the song, "Evangeline" that took us to number one in the whole country was also written by Robbie Robertson. We have indeed come full circle. We also have a cover of

Billy Joe Shaver's song "Blood Is Thicker Than Water," which was kind of the motivation behind this new album. Besides playing bass on the album, Wally applied his expertise in mixing the final tracks with Paul Hampton. That's why the album sounds so good.

A lot of people thought that "Last Ride" was our swan song, as though we were riding off into the sunset. But it's a song about our journey through all the years together. The reference to bringing the curtain down is just part of the song, the story. The inclusion of Jackson Browne and John Fogerty was a direct result of having just watched them both performing at the Jones Beach Theatre. They were my inspiration to write the song "Last Ride."

Last Ride

Rode the Long Island Railroad to Nikon Jones Beach by the sea
Turned 61 years old today and I still feel the Highway calling me
Thinking about the Beatles and how they sent us all out down
　　this road
From 64 to 14 been on this road for half a century
Reminiscing C-Weed years with songs of Jackson Brown in my ears
Fogerty still bitter about the boys in the band all these years
Wanna take that last ride to what might be our final show
Then you can bring that curtain down and let these boys know
　　it's time to go
From a cheap motel in Freeport somewhere up in New York State
Heard the backside of America from a taxi driver harping bout Kuwait
My minds drifting back to our spin doctor brother Bryan at work
Spinning lines about the miles and us free spirit brothers of the road
Reminiscing C-Weed years with songs of Jackson Brown in my ears
Fogerty still bitter bout the boys in the band all these years
Wanna take that last ride to what might be our final show
Then you can bring that curtain down and let these boys know
　　it's time to go

Wanna take that last ride to what might be our final show
Then you can bring that curtain down and let these boys know
   it's time to go

Last Ride was welcomed with open arms by country and Indigenous radio across the country, with the title song and "The Shape I'm In" rising up the charts. It felt good to be back on the charts. On the strength of that album we've been gigging steady. Clint has his own band with his son Riley so Clint's brother Tom fills in with us for some shows.

When I was lying in the hospital after the accident, everyone was coming to see me, family, friends, musicians, politicians, social activists and Indigenous leaders. Elijah Harper leaned over my bed and prayed and wept. Eric Robertson came, of course. Phil Fontaine, John Morrisseau, past president of the Manitoba Métis Federation. They all had the same message for me. "You are alive for a reason. Find out what that reason is. There were five people killed on the road that night. How come you lived that night? Whatever it is, find out and pursue it."

In my hospital bed the idea came to me of a special ceremonial meeting place at The Forks, the traditional meeting spot for Indigenous peoples for thousands of years. I had a vision for South Point at the Forks with the Pow-Wow arbor and a center pole reaching 150 feet into the sky, complete with an Indigenous marketplace surrounding that area, and a Teepee Village on the lower bank across from the main dock of the North side. It would be the finishing touch for The Forks, this huge statement of the significance of the Indigenous people for this particular place on earth called Turtle Island. It is a very spiritual place. I envisioned an interpretive center for the winter months. There are fourteen weekends from May long weekend to September long weekend and they would all feature exhibition Pow-Wows, not competition Pow-Wows, for global tourism and give us an opportunity to display our sense of pride and identity. The thousands of vehicles that drive by over the South Main Bridge would witness the local government's commitment to reconciliation in physical bricks and mortar fashion. This would instill pride in the "Little Guy" Indigenous population as well as the educated and successful Indigenous folk and encourage a sense of IDENTITY.

The exhibition Pow-Wow dancing would feature the different styles of dance, for example grass dancers, jingle dress dancers and so on. Global tourists would pick up a program where all the different styles of dance would be explained along with their significance. They would also be invited to dance in the finale intertribal round dance.

In the vision, I also saw Indigenous people in full regalia paddling huge war canoes that can seat eighteen people out on the river, and buses bringing tourists from the hotels downtown to the docking site by the Louise Bridge. From there, the tourists would board the canoes and have the paddlers bring them upriver, stopping at Fort Gibraltar, have tea and bannock, board the canoes once again and move on upriver. At that point you can see the Canadian Museum for Human Rights and hear the drums from the South Point. The culmination of this excursion would be arriving at the site of the arbor and teepee village; once there, a guide would take the global tourists around the teepee village, the Indigenous marketplace and eventually seat them in the arbor to enjoy the exhibition and participate in the exhibition Pow-Wow.

I just think that this would be amazing. In our culture it is very important that a vision be honoured, that a vision be respected, and most importantly, followed through with.

We, North American Indigenous people, have one of the richest cultures in the world. We have dance, we have visual colours, and we have music, songs, the drums. We have a story; we have a history. It's a hell of a lot more valuable than polar bears. People come from all over the world to see our polar bears. Polar bears? Holy man, Manitoba has got Indians.

For this type of project there has to be true co-operation and partnership. Through my trips to Europe, I learned how Europeans have a high value and respect for North American Indigenous people. They lined up instantly at our table at our first show in Austria to buy our music and various crafts including small dream catchers. My point is that those Austrian people at our first show valued Indian people so much more than we are valued here at home in Canada so they would line up to buy tickets to visit our site at South point here at the Forks. Build it and they will surely come because they have an extremely high value and respect for who we are and what we are about.

I have been waiting for the political and social climate to be ready to get started on this big of a project. I am the visionary; I am not the financer. That will come. I think any great idea, if it is meant to happen, is going to happen. When people see the vision, the financial path will be revealed.

But like anything else, there must be co-operation and reconciliation. There has to be a point where all is reconciled. And if it isn't, then this project will not fly. Until we sit down at the same table and figure out a way to create true, honest and meaningful reconciliation it will never happen. And that reconciliation lies somewhere in the fact that we, the Indigenous First Nations of this land, have a certain value, a great value as Indigenous people to share with the rest of the globe. I think that once we finally partner with Canada in business and say, hey, here is what we bring to the table that will draw thousands and thousands of people from all over the world to our site here at the Forks. Then we will be able to begin to achieve some reconciliation.

These gifts that I have as a leader, spokesperson, role model, writer, poet and singer remain strong within me. It's what drives me onward. These things are bigger than me and I have come to realize that power. In spite of the car crash that left me physically, emotionally and spiritually broken, my focus returned, and I became a driven man again. I believe I was put on this earth to make music and to use my music to influence the success of this global tourism project. It's a huge responsibility, but after trying to outrun it, I have come to understand and embrace it. I've made mistakes but I've admitted them and made amends. I'm not perfect by any stretch. I'm no saint.

At this point in my life, I'm comfortable. Financially, I'm doing about as well as a good lawyer. I don't have the big house and the Mercedes, but I don't need that stuff and never have. I manage the band, take the bookings, pay everyone a decent salary and I look after all the expenses. And we do well.

I don't think I can love again the way I loved Marcie. I may die alone, and I don't mind that thought. I have come to terms with that, although as I write this book, coming to an end of the second decade of 2000, I have ventured into a new relationship, partnership, friendship with a strong Cree woman from Saskatchewan. It is as though the Creator has sent Catherine here to look out for me as I continue my work.

Catherine Buffalo is from the Buffalo clan of Daystar First Nation in Saskatchewan, less than two hours north of Regina. I do not mean that as in the traditional Buffalo Clan. I mean their last name is Buffalo. I have found myself in the middle of a large, beautiful family and have come to love the family matriarch, Catherine's mom Monica, who is eighty-five years young, as well as all her siblings. I missed meeting her father Sydney Buffalo by about ten years as he passed away in January of 2011. I have come to love family get-togethers and the feeling of love and inclusion.

At the end of the day, what do we really need? A home, a place to live in peace and comfort. Food, health, security. You need certain things. But most of all, after it's all said and done, we really need to have the respect of our community. And if you do not have that, then you have nothing. That is my gauge, that is how I measure my worth and my life, by what the community thinks and says about me and what I do. And the only thing that is going to appeal to them is your level of humility. That you can be humble. And you can serve what it is that you are supposed to be doing. And follow the Creator wherever He takes you.

I have always depended on my community. All their support over the years is what kept me going and I am eternally grateful for what they have given me. Now it is my turn to give it back to our community. Those are the things that become important at this stage in my life. It is part of being human. We as a community will come together to "Run As One." It is my vision and our gift.

Gordon, my best friend among my siblings, died in 1995. My older sister Valerie passed away in 1998. My brother Bryan, without whom there wouldn't have been a C-Weed Band, passed away in 2009. He was the man with the plan. It was Bryan's dream to someday write a history book of the C-Weed Band. When I went to see him in the Portage la Prairie hospital, the last words he said to me were "I am going to finish this book, Errol, I am going to finish it." Sadly, he never did. This book here is dedicated to you, Bryan, and all the fans you reached with your press releases and stories for magazines. Rene, one of the younger siblings, passed away in 2009. My older sister Delphine died from cancer as I was writing this book. I miss them all.

A friend of mine, a one-time band mate, can really play the guitar. Fast and clever with his licks. I said to him, "Man, I wish I could play guitar like you" because I can't do any of that fancy guitar stuff. I'm a simple rhythm player. He looked at me and replied, "No, you don't need that. You can write. That's more important than all the hot licks on this guitar. That's why you have us, to do that stuff." It's easy to imitate but much more difficult to create. That's the difference. He can imitate, but I can create. God gave one gift to me and one gift to him. When we share our gifts, a great song is born. I still believe that songs are already written, God plays them in my head, I tune in and write them down. I strum the chords on my guitar and the real musicians in my band help me to fine-tune them.

When I write a song these days I get just as excited as I got when

I was twelve years old back in Eddystone but could not show anyone for fear of being laughed at. We carry so much baggage around when we are young. I believe that songwriting helped set me free. Getting sober and writing "I Wanna Fly" lifted me into flight, away from all the weight of that baggage that I carried for so long as a kid. A very spiritual experience indeed.

The C-Weed Band has provided the musical soundtrack to all the major changes that have taken place in Neeche Country over the last five decades, with a reach from coast to coast to coast. It may have been necessary for us to fly under the radar of major labels and mainstream radio, but we were there. Make no mistake, we were there in the consciousness of the minds of all Canadian fans of music as well as the talking heads of mainstream music and the suits. I am the guy that came to be known as unmanageable and as a result won the very soul of the underground music lovers of the nation.

All along I depended on my brothers for courage. With all the fears and the distress of carrying the stigma of poverty out of the woods of Eddystone, I became battle ready with my brothers behind me for support. Just like when we were playing in the woods of Eddystone as kids, on the road with the band, my brothers followed me anywhere and everywhere into the great unknown to find our date with destiny and brush with fame.

What I have accomplished in my life and what we accomplished as a band, the C-Weed Band, is a good thing. It has given a purpose to my life, a focus and a living. It has also bestowed upon me a platform to speak from where people will listen. It is important to inspire people and I think we have done that. To have come from abject poverty and no hope all the way to the Juno awards and beyond, we have accomplished something, and it is important that I, and my brothers in the band, use that to inspire those that come after us. I am hoping to write another book for the C-Weed band with my two brothers Wally and Don with Clint Dutiaume to share our collective soul with the fans. The real road story version not the sanitized version.

I know I have missed mentioning so many important characters who have passed through my life and have affected the outcome and the quality of my life. You are in my heart and in my soul and you know who you are. Stay gold.

I am the richest guy in the world because I have managed and maneuvered through it all and still maintained the respect of my community. And that is what it was all about anyway.

To paraphrase great man and songwriter—John Lennon—who has served as a true inspiration to me, and the band, over the years, "You may say I'm a dreamer but I'm not the only one; I hope one day you'll join us, and our world will Run As One."

Meegwetch.

ACKNOWLEDGEMENTS

The Beatles for their constant and continuing inspiration for us to be a band.

Robbie Robertson for two timely hit songs "Evangeline" in 1980 and "The Shape I'm in" 2020. 40 years apart.

Our immediate and extended families siblings, cousins, aunts, uncles, in-laws who encouraged us to rise above the obstacles in our path to success.

My two younger brothers Norman and Rene for their tireless work at distributing our music across Canada.

Terry Welsh for his help with my vision for South Point at the Forks.

The Manitoba Metis Federation and especially its current President, David Chartrand and his assistant Don Roulette and Big Al Desjarlais for all their support throughout the years.

All the First Nation communities across Canada and the USA for hosting our concerts over the years. Thank you all.

All the loyal fans for over 50 years who have bought our music and concert tickets and still do.

Aboriginal radio, especially Dave McLeod, who have played our songs throughout the years and still do.

All the great musicians who have played for the C-Weed Band in the absence of my brothers and Clint.

Mitch Daigneault who spent many days constructing the original www.cweedband.com.

My brothers Wally and Don and Clint Dutiaume and Paul Hampton my brothers of the road.

My life long friend "Jigs" Andre Henderson who has been constant in my life, always there to help me with whatever, whenever, and never wanting anything from me. Love you man.

It is hard to be anonymous when I thank AA for all the friends it has given me over the years and kept me alive to help others. As a result I have been 32 years sober.

And of course, my current partner Catherine who organizes my days and keeps me focused. Who loves me and I cherish and love. Thank you for everything you do.

And all the good people who had a hand in the success of the C-Weed Band.